Be you

THE JOURNEY
OF SELF-REALIZATION

Dearest Becky,

*Keep shining your
incredible light* ✦

CHRIS CIRAK

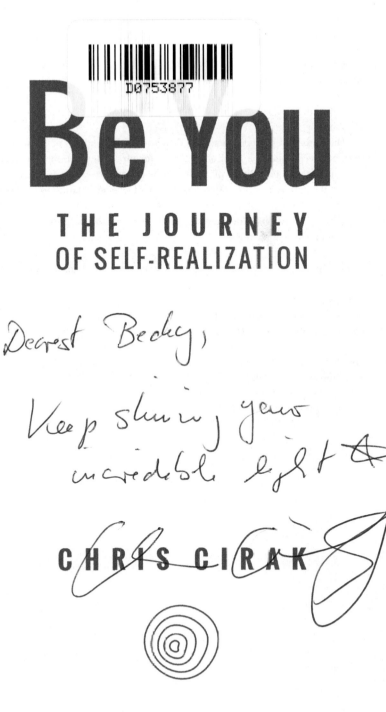

Be You, Chris Cirak, and the tree ring logo are registered trademarks of Cirak Inc.

Editor: Michael Cirak
Cover Design and Photography: Diana Pop
Cover Design and Interior Design: Penina S. Finger

Copyright © 2020 Chris Cirak
1st Edition (Revised 2022)
ISBN: 978-1-7350140-5-0
Website: cirak.com

Dedicated to you.

CONTENTS

PART III

The Big Picture of Being You

ADDENDUM

The Practice of Being You

Be You

PART I

The Essentials of Being You

THE JOURNEY

You are not a random blob of cells. In fact, every part of you *brims* with intention. Your heart never questions why it beats. Your lungs don't get bored pumping air. Your hair doesn't stop growing when you have a bad day. Each sub-atomic particle you consist of knows what role it plays in the great coming together as *you*. If none of your building blocks waver about their purpose, why should you?

Deep down, you know there is someone you're meant to be. Every so often, you catch a glimpse of that someone. It happens when you speak up for yourself, even if it's hard; when you're proud of a job well done, no matter what others say; when you do something for the love of doing it, regardless of the outcome. It happens in those unexpected, almost surreal moments when you look in the mirror and see not your perceived flaws but a person you're amazed by being. *Is that really me?!* Yes, that's really you.

In those distinct moments, you feel that nothing about you is a mistake and that everything about you is meant to be. In those moments, you love life because you love being you. What better way to live life than to be you all the time?

But if being you feels so right, why are you not being you more often? What gets in the way? It's not like you don't want to be more authentic. It's not like you don't want to be more genuine, honest, and compassionate. You want to be all those things and so much more. You want to be someone with a sense of purpose. Someone who is passionate and fulfills their potential. Someone who brings positive change to the world. Someone who never takes the sunrise for granted. And most of all, someone who knows how to love and be loved.

✳

Perhaps you do yoga, keep a gratitude journal, and put positive affirmations on your bathroom mirror. Perhaps you see a therapist and attend workshops on mindfulness and inner healing. Perhaps you've traveled to foreign lands to immerse yourself in ancient wisdom. Whether you've done some of it or none of it, you've reached a point in your life where you're ready to become the person you're meant to be. The single most important thing to remember is:

Who you are is already perfect. It's how you see yourself that gets in the way of your perfection.

✳

There are endless possibilities of how you can live your life
and who you could be. And while it's important to realize
that you could be anyone, it doesn't mean you're meant to
be just anyone. Just like the stars are designed to be stars,
so are you designed to be you. Somewhere deep inside, you
carry your very own blueprint. You can see it whenever
something resonates so deeply that it makes you light up
inside. *That's me!* It's this inner longing to be you that
drives you forward. There isn't a plan you make or a step
you take that isn't motivated by your desire to discover
your most authentic self.

So, where does your authentic self reside? Why is it so
difficult to find? Is it a separate entity that exists outside of
yourself, whose whereabouts are unknown? Of course not.
You are you. You are never not you. You've never taken a
single breath as someone other than yourself.

You cannot find yourself outside of yourself.
You find yourself by being you.

*

No matter how hard you try to leave behind the version of
you that you don't like, in search of a version that you do,
you cannot transform yourself by denying who you are
right now. Your journey is not about becoming someone
you are currently not. Your journey is to be more of who
you already are.

YOUR INNER VOICE

Every moment of every day, you have a choice: To be you, or not to be you. With every choice you make, you're either aligning more with your true self or going against it.

You can tell when you're going against it because that's when life gets difficult. You struggle to find motivation, and you're unclear about your purpose. You question your choices and lack confidence in your actions. Whenever you gain momentum, doubt and fear creep in, and you wind up not following through or jumping to something else. You look around and don't understand why everyone else seems to have their life figured out. You deserve to be just as happy as they are. So, you keep pursuing the things that are supposed to lead to happiness, but no matter how hard you try, no matter how much you achieve, they never do. Life is a hard ride when you're not being you.

In comparison, life is a smooth ride when you *are* being you. You're positive in your outlook and certain in your decisions. You don't feel the need to compare yourself to others because you're comfortable in your own skin. You meet the day head-on with a solution-oriented attitude. There's a calmness about you, and you feel more radiant, confident, and fulfilled. Others want to be in your presence because your *Be You* mojo is inspiring. Good things come to you without even trying, and it feels like life is on your side. Because when you're being you, it is.

Being you is how you build momentum in life. Or rather, how life builds momentum in you.

✳

The best part is: You already know how to be you. There are no special skills you need to acquire. There is no riddle you need to solve. There is no secret door to which you must obtain the password. All you have to do is listen to your inner voice.

Whether you think of it as your intuition, gut instinct, heart, higher self, or inner divinity makes no difference. What matters is that everyone has this voice inside of them. Any situation you find yourself in, it's always there. Your inner voice knows without hesitation, without ambiguity, and without the need for conscious reasoning, what's right for you. It's your fail-safe GPS. As long as you listen, you cannot get lost.

Your inner voice resides in your body, not in your head. Your head is ruled by logic and rationale. It's great for collecting and organizing information, for calculating, strategizing, and executing a plan. It's great for dissecting and analyzing data. Your head is home to your knowledge. But it's not the source of your wisdom.

Think of the trillions of cells that make up who you are. Every one of them knows exactly what to do and how to collaborate with each other. Nothing is random. Every part of you is focused on the task of being you. No wonder your inner voice knows what's true for you. No wonder it can tell when you're being authentic and when you're not.

The more you listen to your inner voice, the less you compare yourself to others. You no longer stress over whether you're doing things *the right way* because you know your way is right for you, and the next person's way is right for them. You always know you're doing your best because being you is being your best. You're not afraid of challenges because you trust your inner voice to speak up at the right time, in the right way. Because it always does. That's its job.

Your inner voice wants you to be you.

It knows who you are in your happiest, most purposeful state. Let it guide you to that place. Be a witness to your life's unfolding in ways you could never imagine, let alone predict. As long as you listen, what is meant to be is meant to happen. And you are meant to happen.

YOUR HEADSPACE

If you can't hear your inner voice or have trouble discerning it, it's because you're in your headspace.

From the moment you're born, you're bombarded by parents, peers, the media, society. Everyone has an opinion on how you should live and who you should be. Everyone thinks they know you. The constant barrage of outside voices fills your headspace to the brim, and you spend most of your time sorting through them, trying to figure out which ones to believe.

By the time you're an adult, you know no other state. In a world designed by and for the headspace, you never get a chance to come out of it to know the difference. You are constantly being asked to formulate a viewpoint on what you like, and what you dislike. What you stand for, and what you oppose. What you believe in, and what you reject.

Without realizing it, you've become conditioned to see the world through the lens of *good or bad* and *right or wrong*.

At first, you don't see the issue with that. You think you're simply voicing your opinions. You might even insist that it's your right to do so. But opinions, attitudes, and perspectives are all forms of mental judgment. And what this constant judging does is keep you deeply entrenched in your headspace, arguing for your beliefs, rationalizing your truths, all the while disconnected from your inner voice.

＊

Before you label something in your mind, it simply exists. But once labeled, it becomes something you can judge. If you pay close attention, you can tell how you can't think of anything without also thinking of it as *I like or I dislike.* Judging is such an integral part of thinking that you forget that nothing in life is inherently good or bad.

Things happen, whether you have an opinion about them or not. The happening, by itself, is neither good nor bad until your mind makes it so. As long as you live in your headspace, you judge everything you encounter.

The effort of continuous judging is enormous. To see something as right, you must first see everything else as wrong. To accept something as true, you must reject all else as false. Your mind cannot help but weigh the pros and cons of every step you take, always looking to convince itself that the path you're on is the right one to be on. This constant judging of life as *for me or against me* is an arduous, thankless task. But it's not flawed behavior. It's just how your mind works.

When you're in your headspace, you're continuously comparing yourself to the world around you. That's why you care so much about what others think. You need their approval to feel confident. You need them to celebrate you to feel like a success. You need their love so you can feel lovable. This is what makes life so complicated. How you feel is dependent on the world around you. When someone agrees with you, you feel validated. When someone disagrees with you, you feel rejected. When something benefits you, you're thrilled. When it doesn't benefit you, it makes you upset.

When you rely on the world for how you feel, your life is a roller coaster that never ends.

*

In contrast, your inner voice doesn't rely on comparison, so it doesn't need to make others wrong to know what's right for you. It doesn't need to label one thing as true and everything else as false. Rather, wisdom arises from a much deeper place where *everything* is true. *Everyone* has a right to be. Your inner voice recognizes:

Your inner truth does not compete with the truth of others.

Whenever you see injustice in the world, it's committed by people who are disconnected from their inner voice.

Only when you're lost in the duel of competing voices in your headspace is it possible to rationalize doing harm to others, as well as to yourself.

You don't need to be one of those people. They don't know any better, but you do. Come out of your headspace and trust your inner voice. There couldn't be a better guide to harmony with life, love, and yourself.

THOUGHT AWARENESS

As domineering as your headspace may be, you can free yourself from its grip. Yes, you heard right. This wild, hyperactive mind of yours can be tamed. Or rather, it can be reset to its natural state of equanimity. Coming out of constant reactivity to a world gone mental is your primary obstacle to living a healthy and purpose-driven life.

The key to freeing yourself from incessant thinking is to become more aware of your thoughts. To practice *thought awareness*, try this exercise: With your eyes and mouth closed, put your attention on the incoming and outgoing breath at the entrance of your nose. See how long you can keep your attention there without losing focus. Try it now for one minute.

The first thing you realize is that the mind is incredibly fickle. Within seconds, your attention begins to waver, you lose track of your breath, and you get lost in thought about other things. The habit of incessantly jumping from one random thought to the next is so strong, even when you're fully aware of it, you can't help yourself.

At first, it can be incredibly frustrating - even shocking - to realize you can't keep your mind focused for more than a few seconds on something as basic as your breath. If your mind's attention were a matchstick, it couldn't keep steady long enough to light a candle. But then the bigger dilemma sinks in. Has it occurred to you that this is the same mind you rely on for making life-altering decisions? The same mind you depend on for your identity, and to give your life meaning? If your mind is this fickle, how can you trust it for something as critical as guiding you through life?

You think you can control life, but you can't even control your mind.

Notice how often you get lost in thought. It happens even when you're doing things that deserve your fullest attention, such as driving a car, attending a concert, or taking a class. Easily, five, ten, twenty minutes or more go by, completely absent in thought. When you come out of it, it feels like you're re-emerging from a dense fog.

Where have you been? Your body is still here, but it feels like you've been gone the entire time, wrestling with thoughts about *should haves* and *could haves,* going down rabbit holes of *what if* and *why me,* or just randomly pondering things that don't impact you whatsoever. Sometimes your thoughts become so erratic and absurd, even your imagination thinks it's time to put an end to it.

Drifting off into thoughts happens so fast, you don't even notice it until you snap back out of it. But within no time, and without warning, you drift off again. This pattern keeps repeating all day long and into the night. You can spend most of your life lost in thought.

*

Fortunately, you are not doomed to live life in the noisy caverns of your mind. With a daily practice of thought awareness, your mind starts to calm down, and the length of time you're able to stay out of your headspace increases. It might only be a few extra seconds at first, but you can't expect to gain independence from your thoughts overnight. You've been believing them all your life. The pull of your mind is so strong, one innocuous thought can whisk you away and turn into an hour-long mental excursion.

Practicing thought awareness doesn't just help you come out of mental reactivity. It also shifts the center of your awareness to your body, making your sensations the point of connection which everyday life. The resulting deprioritization of your headspace paves the way for one of the most important revelations of your life:

You are not your thoughts.

The more you practice thought awareness, the more it sinks in that just because thoughts arise doesn't mean you have to believe them. The problem is, when you're in your headspace, you do. You identify with them. That's what gives them power over you. But once you become aware of your thoughts, you realize - as all-important as they make themselves out to be - you can easily just let them go.

*

It's important to understand that progress in your thought awareness practice doesn't come from focusing on how long you're able to keep your attention on your breath. Rather, it's the number of times you come back to your breath after drifting off that diffuses your reactivity and weakens your mind's grip on you.

Don't get frustrated for getting lost in thought. Celebrate each time you become aware of it.

You can practice thought awareness anywhere, anytime throughout the day. It's your go-to strategy for whenever you feel anxious, agitated, troubled, confused, unfocused, uncreative, depleted, bored, or generally unbalanced. All these feelings come from spending too much time in your headspace and not enough time in your body.

Let the benefits of your thought awareness practice speak for themselves. Let your experience determine how long and how often is suitable for you. No doubt, it can be challenging at first to wrestle control away from your mind. Plus, living in a world designed to elicit reactions from you doesn't make it easier. Just know that no matter how tough the going gets, your inner voice is only a breath away.

FILTERED REALITY

To deepen your thought awareness practice, it's helpful to understand why your mind keeps drifting off.

Your mind needs to know things. That's its job. It can't just let the unknown be. Not knowing makes it anxious, fearful, and stressed. Your mind is designed to analyze, explain, define things - to make the unknown known. The need to know is the core experience of living in your head.

You can see this in your everyday life. The next time you're in the shower, take a moment to notice what you're thinking about. In all likelihood, it's not how great it feels to have water pouring over you or how satisfying it is to get clean. Instead, you're thinking about what comes next. That's because your mind fears the unknown. It's always looking for the next unknown moment, trying to fill it with something it already knows. Essentially, your mind is obsessed with predicting the future.

In contrast, the past is much easier to deal with. What has already happened is known, and that puts your mind at ease. But the future drives your mind nuts because there's nothing there. It's about as unknown as can be.

This is where the outside voices in your headspace come into play, many of which claim to know the future. You're told if you study hard, you can expect to land a great job, attract a great partner, create a happy family, take nice vacations, save up money, and retire in style. Your mind takes this story, or any variation of it, and projects it into the future. And voilà! Your unknown future becomes the known. It's so easy, it's almost too good to be true!

✳

It turns out it is. Severe complications arise when the future you expect doesn't match the future that happens. And it never does. Once your life gets going, the details start to fill in. The initial story turns into a very different reality. You might get into another school, find interest in a different career, fall in love when you least expect it or not at all, have more children than you can afford or none at all, realize you hate your job, burn through your nest egg and start all over again, rarely take a vacation or turn your whole life into one, discover a hidden talent, find a hidden treasure, battle an unknown disease, take care of an ailing parent, make a ton of money in the stock market, lose a ton of money in the stock market, and start all over again - again. Life can take any number of roads. Ultimately, that's what makes it so special. Things only get dramatic when you insist it should take a specific one.

Expecting life to unfold according to the story you tell yourself means you no longer see reality as it is. You see it through the filters of what you want it to be. You see a filtered reality. Filtered reality is the primary source of all frustration, disappointment, and unhappiness in your life. You're always comparing what is happening to what you think *should* be happening. And when the two don't match, you get upset.

The reason they don't match is not that life is being mean to you. The reason is simply that it's impossible to know what an experience feels like until you actually experience it. Until then, it's merely an expectation. Your mind cannot know the future. When it gets here, it's *always* different than what you expect.

Reality isn't real until it is.

✳

Remember your fickle mind, how it keeps drifting off into thoughts? They are primarily thoughts about your filtered reality. You keep thinking about what you want and what you don't want. What you like and what you dislike. You keep revisiting your plans and whether you should do things differently. You keep projecting your next steps to stay on top of expectations. Because if you let life happen on its own accord - the mind says - it's bound to be limited and unfulfilling.

But when you come out of your headspace, you realize the opposite is the case. It's your filtered reality that is limited and unfulfilling. It doesn't take much to see why. Life contains far more variations than you can possibly imagine. There are far more energies at play than you can ever comprehend. Your life is a much greater adventure than you could ever predict. Even your biggest dreams are still limited to what your mind can make up.

You cannot manifest your greatest life from your mind. It's too small and anxious a place.

Practicing thought awareness helps you stay out of filtered reality so you can respond to what is actually happening in front of you. Life, unfiltered, is incredibly simple and uncomplicated. There is no right or wrong. There are no *should haves, could haves,* and *what-ifs.* Each moment arrives and brings with it all that is possible, including that which your mind deems impossible.

Stay connected to each new moment and stay fresh, inspired, intrigued, and tuned into the infinite ways that love, joy, and abundance can come to you. All you have to do to take part in this reality, is see it as it is.

SEPARATENESS

When you're in your headspace you experience yourself as separate from the world around you. Instead of letting life happen, you insist that it happen according to your plans. You think your filtered reality is better than the reality in front of you. But all you're doing is creating friction by limiting yourself to what you already believe. All you're doing is taking yourself out of the flow.

Whenever you label something as *good*, you're also labeling everything else in that space as *bad*. Whenever you say *I like that*, you're also saying that you *don't* like everything else you looked at to arrive at that conclusion.

If you look closely, you can see how the constant judging reinforces a sense of separation. Each time you judge you're saying *I'm over here, and what I like is over there*. Or *I'm over here and what I dislike is over there*. All day long, your mind is engaged in an incessant stream of judgments that create thousands of little impressions of separateness. Whether you judge things positively or negatively makes no difference. Your mind's function of labeling inherently isolates you from the world around you.

Your mind sees itself as separate from everything it defines.

Feeling separate is at the root of all your fears, all your loneliness, all your unrest. It makes you feel insignificant and small, that you're incomplete and not enough, and that you're all alone trying to survive in a big scary world.

It makes you focus on differences over uniqueness, borders over unity. It creates a world starved of love and kindness and generates the illusion of scarcity on a planet overflowing with abundance. The alliance of life borders on the absurd. There is no end to how all the shapes, sizes, colors, sounds, tastes, and textures interact with each other in harmony, in a kind of holy dance. But you cannot participate in the sanctity of life - nor can you recognize it in yourself - when you feel separate from it.

✳

Your mind thinks the formula for happiness is to cling to *good* things and resist *bad* things. It doesn't realize that judging both separates you from - and limits you to - the objects of your judgments. Whether you label something as *good* or *bad* makes no difference. Both become equal components of your filtered reality.

Thus, you can never get away from the things you don't want. Once a judgment enters your headspace, it becomes fused to your mental map of what you think exists. Not wanting something cements it as part of the content of your life, as much as the things you desire.

Can you see how, if you didn't judge something, it couldn't upset you? It would have no power over you. When you judge things, you give away your power.

✳

Ultimately, all judgment is self-judgment. Whenever you say someone is *wrong*, you're judging yourself to be right. When you say someone is *dumb*, you're judging yourself to be smart. Every judgment directed at others is a reflection of how you feel about yourself. You're always judging life from the perspective of *me*.

Indeed, *me* is your judging mind's favorite target. You can judge yourself for the way you look, think, talk, and walk, for where you come from, what you're doing, and where you're going. You even judge yourself for judging yourself. More often than not, you are your own worst critic.

Judging profoundly impacts your emotional wellbeing. Whenever you judge anything, you align yourself with the energy of your judgment. Try it right now. Think of someone you consider to be an *idiot*.

How does that make you feel? Not good, right? That's because when you call someone an idiot, you generate that feeling of what it means to be an idiot inside of you. By the time you speak it, you're already stewing in negativity. In other words, whenever you judge others, you harm yourself first. By calling someone an idiot, you also become one.

Most judgments floating around in your head aren't even your own. Many you've inherited from your family lineage, tracing back countless generations. Others you've absorbed from your social group, and others still from society. You take on these judgments as your own, and they dictate how you react to the world. This is how both at the individual and collective levels, ingrained judgments are blindly perpetuated, preventing people and nations from finding peace within themselves and with each other.

✳

As long as you're in your headspace, you don't see your separateness because being in your headspace *is* the separateness. Only by coming out of it and connecting with your body can you dissolve the sense of distance to others and recognize the common humanity shared by all.

Your journey of self-realization is the path to unity with yourself and the world around you. As your separateness decreases, connectedness takes hold. Creativity, wisdom, and abundance start to flow. There is no greater experience than to be part of everything that exists. Be you and be one.

STUCK FEELINGS

Life is continuously in motion. It never stands still. With each breath you take, the sun has traveled, the oceans have shifted, the grass has grown. From the perspective of a still observer, everything is on its way in and on its way out. Everything is coming and going.

You are that still observer. All day long, things enter and exit your experience. Along with those experiences come feelings. The natural flow of these feelings is also to come and go. But most of the time, that's not what happens. Instead of coming and going, they get stuck inside of you.

Feelings get stuck when you cling to the ones you like and resist the ones you don't like.

At first, this seems like normal behavior. You cling to positive feelings because you like feeling them. You don't want to lose them. You want them to stay. But when good feelings fade, it causes you stress, anxiety, and depression.

Conversely, you resist negative feelings by pushing them away. You think pushing them away gets rid of them. But they gnaw at you from the inside, causing you stress, anxiety, and depression.

As stuck feelings accumulate, they have a direct adverse effect on your mental, emotional, and physical well-being. Your outlook on life dims. Your energy dwindles. Little things annoy you way more than they should. Making decisions feel heavy, like you're carrying around a weight. That's because you are. Stuck feelings create energetic blockages that interrupt your natural free-flowing state. If left unaddressed, they eventually surface as illness.

✳

Fortunately, you can learn to release stuck feelings. The trick is remarkably simple: you observe them. Observing them doesn't mean not feeling them. On the contrary, it means experiencing them fully, without reacting to them. You react to feelings by clinging to the ones you like and resisting the ones you don't. That's what keeps them stuck.

Feeling your feelings and reacting to your feelings are two different things.

The key to learning to observe your feelings without reacting to them is to recognize that all feelings show up as sensations in your body. When you fall in love, you might feel butterflies in your stomach. When you're scared, the hair on the back of your neck might bristle. When you get angry, your heart might be pounding in your chest. Every feeling has a corresponding sensation in your body that you can learn to observe.

By observing sensations, you release stuck feelings back into the flow.

To let this sink in fully, it's helpful to understand the signal chain. First, your five senses engage with the world around you and send signals to your brain. Next, your brain interprets those signals based on its conditioning and generates feelings. Finally, you experience those feelings as sensations somewhere in your body. Normally, sensations would arise and pass, if you were purely feeling them. But when you react to your feelings with *I like* and *I don't like,* it causes them to get stuck. Again, your feelings and your reaction to them are two different things.

Seeing it broken down like this gives way to one of the most pivotal insights in your journey. You realize that most of the difficulties in life come from your reaction to your feelings, not the feelings themselves, and that most feelings are very manageable as long as they're free to come and go.

It's not things that happen that upset you. It's your reaction to things that happen that upsets you.

*

The first step in releasing stuck feelings is to look for where they show up in your body. Negative stuck feelings might show up as heaviness in your chest, constriction in your throat, or discomfort in your stomach region. They might show up as pressure behind your eyes or throbbing in your head. They might show up as a sharp, pinpoint pain or a broad, simmering sensation. Similarly, positive stuck feelings might show up as light-headedness, a tingling in your chest, or a glowing feeling throughout your body. Whether positive or negative, all stuck feelings show up as physical sensations *somewhere*. All you have to do to release them is to learn to observe them.

✳

Go ahead and try it right now. Think of a difficult situation you're currently dealing with, something or someone you feel triggered by. Sit with those thoughts until you notice feeling triggered. Now look for where you feel it in your body and put your unbiased attention there.

The first thing you notice is your immediate resistance to what you're feeling. The tendency to want to push away the discomfort is deeply ingrained. It's almost an instant reaction. But it's precisely this reaction that causes your feelings to get stuck.

Now, come back to where you feel the sensations and continue to observe them, without pushing anything away. If you lose focus, simply notice your attention has drifted, and bring it back to the sensations. Sound familiar?

This is where the power of your thought awareness practice comes back into play. Your ability to focus on your breath is the same ability that helps you focus on your sensations. Self-observation becomes the main instrument in your toolbox of self-regulation and self-healing.

*

Keep observing your sensations for about a minute. Notice a change in the quality or intensity of the sensations? Or a shift in the area from which they radiate? If so, it means stuck feelings are starting to break free. By no longer reacting to your feelings, you're actually feeling them, and by actually feeling them, you're letting them go.

Should you experience an initial increase in the intensity of your sensations, no need to be alarmed. It's happening because you're no longer pushing your feelings away. Instead, you're giving them space to be. Eventually, the intensity subsides, and the discomfort diminishes - until something truly remarkable happens: The sensations dissolve. They're no longer there. The emotional charge has left your body. You instantly feel lighter and brighter. Congratulations! You've just released your stuck feelings back into the flow. Both you and the feelings are free.

*

Surprisingly easy, right? Now you can apply this method to all stuck feelings, including positive ones. The challenge with positive stuck feelings is that you like feeling them, so you may find it harder to let them go. But if you don't let them go, they, too, keep you out of the flow, enslaved to your mind's reactivity. There is never anything to be gained from stuck feelings. Observe them and release them.

Depending on how stuck a particular feeling is, the amount of observation time needed to release it can vary. But with enough practice, even the toughest emotional clog can be cleared through non-reactive self-observation. Your feelings are meant to come and go.

The sooner you release something that's bothering you, the better. Each day brings new situations that prompt reactions from you. New stuck feelings get piled on top of old ones from yesterday. Before you know it, you can no longer remember all the situations you've reacted to.

The good news is, you don't need to know which past events have caused certain stuck feelings. In fact, analyzing just pulls you back into your headspace. All that matters is observing your sensation as they show up right now.

By releasing the top layers of stuck feelings, the bottom layers rise to the surface all on their own. Remember, the natural movement of all feelings is to come and go. That's why hurt feelings naturally diminish over time. But now, you don't need to wait, nor do you need to live in fear of getting hurt again. You can release yourself from the fear grip of all difficult emotions.

Your journey of self-realization is a journey of self-healing.

*

It should be noted that some stuck feelings can be very challenging. If you ever feel overwhelmed by what comes up for you, don't hesitate to seek outside help. Asking for support from family, friends, or healthcare professionals is part of your commitment to self-care. You're not showing weakness. You're honoring yourself. You're choosing to feel better, and asking others for help is part of your journey.

*

Set aside time each day to observe your sensations and release stuck feelings. Nothing has a more immediate and lasting positive impact on your well-being and quality of life. How much time you allocate to your practice is for you to determine, but the benefits speak for themselves. Your outlook brightens, your productivity increases. Difficult situations no longer irritate you as much as before. You're able to keep your composure even in the most triggering conditions. You're more balanced, relaxed, and likely to come out of patterned behavior. Your ability to think clearly and critically skyrockets. Your feelings flow freely, unburdened by stuck energy from the past. A deep sense of gratitude arises from experiencing yourself in this simplicity. You realize that life is simple until you make it complicated, that your natural state is to be free of emotional burden, and that even the most difficult feelings are a lot less challenging when you allow them to pass.

All this time, you've been blaming life for being difficult, wishing it was easy. When, in reality, life is easy, but you've been making it difficult.

＊

By letting your feelings come and go, you become part of the coming and going. That's where you're one with life. Every emotion that passes through you makes you a deeper, wiser, more compassionate person. Instead of clinging and resisting, let your feelings transform you into the person you're meant to be.

TRIGGERS

Nobody likes feeling triggered. And for good reason! Feeling triggered leads to irritation, upset, anger, sadness. Often you don't even know why you feel triggered. Certain people just rub you the wrong way. The easiest course of action is to blame others, push away your feelings, and keep avoiding the things that trigger you. Or so it seems.

As is so often the case, the easy route is not in your best interest. By avoiding triggers, you avoid the core feedback mechanism of life. Triggers are life's way of showing you where you harbor resentment, anger, fear, or lack. In other words, they point to stuck feelings. Of course, nobody likes being reminded of where they have work to do. But as with all of life, resistance is futile. Everything has a purpose.

Triggers are here to help you heal.

Triggers come in all sizes. Some are overwhelmingly big, like the loss of a loved one. Others are annoyingly small, like when you've misplaced your keys. Triggers have a sneaky way of showing up when you least expect it, right when you're certain that peace and quiet are finally here. But the only thing that's certain is that as long as you carry stuck feelings, triggers are bound to find you.

✳

It's oddly poetic that the very things that annoy you are the things that provide you with insight about yourself. That's not life being a pain in your neck. That's how it's supposed to work. Life is pushing you towards greater authenticity and well-being. In fact, you don't have to sit in lotus pose or perform a hundred thousand sun salutations. You don't have to renounce your belongings or go live on a desert island. You don't have to do anything differently than what you're doing right now. Just live your life, and triggers come right to you.

Even if you don't embrace triggers as an opportunity for insight, even if the topic of self-growth doesn't resonate whatsoever, eventually, you get tired of repeating the same patterns. Reacting to the same old situations in the same old ways wears you down. Slowly, but surely, the idea starts to build that there must be a better way to live life than to be in constant reaction to it; that feeling triggered is telling you something about yourself; and that there must be something you can do about it.

There comes a turning point when you realize the world isn't doing anything to you. You are doing everything to yourself. You're not at the mercy of your environment. You're at the mercy of how you react to your environment. The people and situations that trigger you are not to blame. They're here to help you become more aware of all the ways you're stuck.

∗

Triggers don't only point to negative stuck feelings. They can also reveal positive ones. Achieving a personal goal makes you flushed with excitement, and deservedly so. You should always celebrate your successes. But difficulties arise when you cling to the high. You wind up feeling empty and disengaged from your everyday life, yearning for experiences in the past, wanting today to be different, hoping that tomorrow is like yesterday.

Ultimately, triggers are a reflection of something that's misaligned within. This is how life is your mirror. It has no agenda for you to be needlessly upset. It doesn't want you to suffer. In fact, it wants you to come out of the misery of not being you. It wants you to release stuck feelings so you can return to your natural, free-flowing state. Until then, embrace your triggers. And remember:

Life wants you to be you.

CLEAR ACTION

Clear action represents the best-case scenario for handling any given situation. It's a shift in perspective from *what's best for me* to *what's best for the situation.*

That doesn't mean you neglect your own well-being. On the contrary, what's best for the situation is also best for you. Remember, how you react to the world is a reflection of any stuck feelings you carry. Rather than resist, fight, and blame your circumstances, it's in your best interest to collaborate with them because, essentially, they are you.

To be at peace with the world you must be at peace with yourself.

Take, for example, a situation where another car takes a parking spot you've been waiting for. You could respond in one of two ways. You could get upset, honk, shout, and create a scene. Or you could accept the spot is now taken and move on to the next one with minimal delay.

It's the exact same situation, with two very different outcomes. In the first instance, you resist what is happening, insist on what you think *should* be happening, berate the other driver, and spend the rest of the day stewing in reactivity, even if you wind up getting the spot. In the second scenario, you flow with the circumstances and barely miss a beat.

Your mental state sets the tone for the situation. If you respond from reactivity, you accuse the other driver of being rude, that they deserve to be reprimanded. But if you stay equanimous, guided by your inner voice, you know that dishing out negativity only hurts yourself. Remember, when you scold others, you generate that energy within yourself first. No matter how right you may be, the reality is your day is ruined, not from having lost a parking spot, but from your reaction to it.

✳

There is no objective interpretation of any situation. It's always shaped by how you respond to it. The next person experiences the same event based on *their* reactive makeup. It becomes clear that your physical circumstances and how you respond to them are two separate things. The problem is that growing up in a head-centric world, you become conditioned to *re*-act rather than take action from a place of clarity.

Action based on reactivity only leads to confrontation. Action based on your inner voice, however, is *clear action*. Clear action is the fastest and most effective way to resolve any situation. It's always tied to how things are and not how you want them to be.

When you help each moment unfold perfectly into the next, nothing is guesswork. Everything is unfiltered and real. You see situations as they are, and your inner voice guides you through them. That's how simple and effortless life is supposed to be.

As you gain confidence in your ability to respond to circumstances as they are, you find you have little use for things like hope, luck, coincidence, or even divine intervention. That's because you're no longer trying to control life. You're no longer concerned with outcomes because you're taking care of matters as they arise.

Not focusing on outcomes doesn't mean you aimlessly float through life. It doesn't mean you accept whatever may come. On the contrary, every instance of clear action leads to clear results. Clear results, in turn, inspire more clear action. A life of clarity and positive momentum starts to build. Your journey takes shape organically, without you even trying.

By taking clear action, the bigger picture reveals itself all on its own.

✳

Never take action unless it's clear action. If you don't feel clear, perhaps you need more information. In that case, do research. Research can be part of clear action. That's when your mind is a great tool. Absorb the information, let it sink into your body, and let your truth arise from there.

No action can also be clear action. There is no universally right or wrong way to respond to any given situation. Everyone contributes to the world differently.

Let what's right for you be right for you and what's right for others be right for them.

Once clear action reveals itself, it's essential that you act. If you don't act and simply carry on making decisions from your headspace, you can't expect clear results. Only later on, you might look back, remember hearing your inner voice, and regret not listening to it.

Should this happens, don't be hard on yourself. Your mind always sees clearly in hindsight. In fact, that's the only time it sees clearly. The most important thing is never to blame yourself for winding up in a tough spot. There's nothing to be gained from *could have* or *should have*. Instead, look for the lesson contained in the experience and take clear action from there. Ultimately, it's through clear action that you unravel the conditioning of your mind. Instead of blindly repeating old patterns, you're now able to reflect on old behavior and bring positive, lasting change to yourself and the world.

∗

There is great clarity contained in the coming and going of life. Embrace each precious moment for what it is because it's already gone by the time you form an opinion about it. Take clear action and facilitate more of the flow, and in return, the flow facilitates more of you.

SELF-REALIZATION

In the outer world, there are places you're familiar with, places you're unfamiliar with, and places you don't even know exist. The more familiar you are with a specific place, the more it feels like home.

Your inner world is no different. It consists of parts you're more familiar with, parts you're less familiar with, and parts you don't even know exist. The journey of self-realization is to feel at home in all of your parts.

You can't be yourself if you don't know yourself.

*

It's both an ironic and divine feature of your world that *not* knowing yourself is what propels you forward. Ironic because your mind is all about knowing. Divine because you get to experience the miracle of each new moment. Every part of you in which you haven't realized yourself yet contains both the anguish of not being you and the infinite longing to be more of you.

Self-realization is the process of realizing who you are. You are never *not* experiencing this process. Every moment of every day, life is pushing you to know yourself better. More specifically, *you* are the one doing the pushing. Life is just a mirror. Stuck feelings are the fuel of your evolution.

If it feels like you're taking detours instead of the direct route, that's your headspace talking. It loves to analyze and criticize you for making mistakes, saying you should know better. It quickly forgets that you're a more realized person now, precisely because of how you've responded to things in the past. Ultimately, there's no reason to fault yourself for anything, ever. As always, the core lesson of *not* being you is to prompt you to become more of you. You haven't failed. You haven't taken a wrong turn. You're always in the perfect spot, doing what you're supposed to be doing.

You're always you, doing the best you can.
There is no other way.

✳

Resist the urge to plan out your life for fear you might go down the wrong road. Right and wrong only exist when you listen to your mind, focused on outcomes. In the great unfolding of your life, you spend most of your time veering off your path. Each time you veer and come back, you grow in clarity, awareness, and alignment. You become more of you. The process of life is not one to sit still. Your journey is meant to go through a field of experiences.

Detours and excursions aren't just part of your journey, they are your journey.

✳

Everything you experience puts you in touch with your feelings. How you respond to your feelings is how you participate in and contribute to, the flow of life. When your feelings stay stuck, you generate friction within yourself and your environment. But by releasing them, you contribute free-flowing energy and harmony to the world.

As you become more realized, so does the world.

Less realized energy, longing to become *more* realized energy, is the engine behind life's continuous expansion. Everything you do in the physical dimension is motivated by this pull. You buy things to experience abundance. You fall in love to experience unity. You set goals to experience fulfillment. You're always in the process of replacing what you hope to experience with the actual experience of it.

That's why you're supposed to buy shiny things and be enamored by them. You're supposed to fall in love and promise each other foreverness. You're supposed to rise to the highest highs and fall to the lowest lows. You're supposed to experience all those things because it's not about the things. It's not about reaching goals or achieving outcomes. It's about realizing yourself along the way.

*

You can never call a person realized or unrealized. Self-realization is not an on/off switch. It's not a badge that grants you access to the exclusive *Club of Realized Beings*, where life serves you champagne and caviar. Rather, self-realization is the unstoppable process of your evolution. It's why you're here. As long as there are parts of you that you're unfamiliar with, your journey continues.

But don't fret. You're doing great. There's no such thing as the perfect plan. It's all in the process. Stuck feelings manifest your circumstances, bringing you the lessons you're ready for. You're always in the right spot to realize yourself more. You cannot be anywhere else.

The best roadmap for life is living it.

Ultimately, being more realized doesn't make your life easy. It helps you not make it more difficult. Life is defined by its challenges. Yet, even the hardest times are much more manageable when you remember that everything is meant to come and go, and that underneath the layers of stuck feelings, life is incredibly simple and uncomplicated, and you are already perfect. So, keep living your life. Your fully realized self awaits.

PART II

Insights
of Being You

MANIFESTATION

The idea of getting what you want, simply by desiring it, has universal appeal. It's a powerful feeling to imagine that unlimited prosperity and abundance are at your fingertips and that all you have to do is think it into existence.

But manifestation is not a stand-alone activity you engage in whenever you want something special to happen. It's not a ritual performed behind closed doors. It's not an altered state you achieve that unlocks secret capabilities. It's not a special skill, reserved for the fortunate few.

You're *always* manifesting. You manifest by being you. You manifest by not being you. You manifest your reality, right now, constantly, all the time. You can't *not* manifest. Manifesting is being, and being is manifesting. You don't have to learn to manifest. You are already an expert at it.

The question is not, how do I manifest? The question is, what am I manifesting?

✳

What you manifest on the outside is always a reflection of your degree of alignment on the inside. When you're being you, you feel abundant. Thus, you manifest abundance. When you're *not* being you, you feel empty. Therefore, you manifest lack. Everything around you at this very moment is a reflection of how much or how little you are being you.

To be you is to be in receiving mode. You're listening to your inner voice, responding to circumstances, taking clear action, and harvesting clear results. In contrast, when you're *not* being you, you're in steering mode. You're always in resistance, feelings keep getting stuck, and reactivity keeps interrupting the flow of abundance that life sends your way.

To be you is to be abundant. Not to be you is to experience lack.

✳

But the mind struggles mightily with attracting abundance. Growing up in a world based on fear and lack, you become conditioned to believe scarcity is prevalent and you must will your way to getting anything. But trying to manifest from your headspace is the ultimate exercise in futility. Remember your fickle mind? You think you know what you want. But your attention keeps jumping around, reacting to one thing after another. *I want this! No, I want that!* Your mind needs to see proof, so when there's no immediate evidence, it loses faith. *I don't see it, so it's not happening.*

And off you go chasing the next idea and the next plan. You can never participate in life's abundance when your mind is all over the place. The world can never catch up to your inconsistent desires. All it can do is mirror the chaos.

When abundance *does* show up in the external, it doesn't just appear out of nowhere. Abundance is always there. You just don't see it when you're not being you. Manifestation is never about creating something out of nothing. It's making yourself available to receive all that's already there.

You experience as much abundance as you're open to let in.

The great irony is that once the world catches up to your fullness, you no longer need the world to make you feel full. You're already as fulfilled as can be. That's when you become truly free to enjoy things while they're here because you don't fear the thought of them being gone.

✳

The hardest part for your mind to grasp is that the more you want something you don't have, the more you create resistance to receiving it. On the outside, you may be saying *I want this!* But on the inside, you're reinforcing the feeling of not having it. As such, words often belie how you really feel inside. But how you feel is the primary place from which you manifest.

That's why you can't manifest abundance when you complain about lack; why it's hard to feel healthy when you take so many pills; why you can't find peace when you consume unsettling news; why you can't meet your special someone when you fear being alone. You're giving your attention to all the things you don't want in your life, so those are the things you get.

Whenever you want something, but are unsure of how to get it - or you're sure of how to get it, but don't know if you want it - you know you're caught in the endless loop of your analytical mind. When that happens, take a step back and look for the last thing that resonates with you. Look for that feeling of *that's me!* Stay connected to that feeling and build your life around it. Never let it go. Let that feeling guide your expansion.

As long as you stay connected to the feeling of you, you're never not in a state of fulfillment.

If you look at your life and find that nothing resonates, no need to despair. Knowing what doesn't resonate is just as valuable as knowing what does. Maybe even more. Remember, you can't realize yourself by sitting on the couch. You find yourself by doing things. Most of your journey consists of experiencing things that don't resonate, pointing you to things that do. Your inner voice knows when to say *no*, as much as when to say *yes*.

*

Abundance manifests from the joy of being you. Just look at nature if you still need proof. Everything thrives on being itself. The result is a world full of abundance piled on top of more abundance. Life is the abundance train that never stops. You jump on board by being you.

To manifest your brightest future, pay close attention to how you feel *right now*. Being you now informs the quality of each subsequent moment, and that's how the path to your happy self unfolds.

You manifest your happy future one happy moment at a time.

Every time you choose to be you, you feel a little more confident, more powerful, more complete. A deep sense of abundance arises and fills you to the brim. As long as you listen to your inner voice, you can only keep expanding. You no longer wait for the world to fulfill you because you already feel the way you want to be feeling. Build on that feeling of being you, for you are the ultimate manifestation.

SELF-LOVE

The more you realize yourself, the more you realize you love yourself. It becomes clear that loving yourself is your natural state.

The journey of self-realization is the journey of self-love.

Not loving yourself makes everything difficult. Instead of focusing on the things you've accomplished, you criticize yourself for the things you haven't. Instead of being comfortable in your own skin, you pressure yourself to look a certain way, act a certain way, and achieve certain things. You're always comparing yourself to others, looking for the next thing to fix about yourself, never taking the time to appreciate who you really are and how far you've come. Not loving yourself is so hard, so abusive, it makes you wonder why you keep doing it.

If there is a lack of love in your life, the primary reason is you're looking for love from others instead of finding it in yourself. You demand that the people around you show up for you in precisely the right way, using the right words, doing the right things, at the right time, so you feel loved in all the ways you don't love yourself. And if that isn't enough, you also need them to promise to love you *forever*. Forever - that's how long you plan on not loving yourself.

You can never win in conditional love. Every time your conditions are not met, it brings up fear of abandonment, of feeling unwanted and unlovable. You might exert even more control over others to meet your needs for affection. But no matter how much attention you demand from the world, that perfect, everlasting love remains elusive. All that your externalized needs have done is create pressure that is bound to boil over.

But this is exactly how it's supposed to happen. You're supposed to experience the end of conditional love. You're supposed to wake up and realize that no one can love you exactly the way you need to be loved, let alone forever. And most importantly:

No one can make you love yourself.

*

The more you seek completion in the world around you, the more you realize that's not where it's found. Each time you feel let down by others, it points to stuck feelings inside that make you feel like you're not enough. It reminds you that you're the still observer that life is passing through, that your entire perception of reality is happening within you, and that the only thing permanent in your experience is *you*.

Life is all about learning to love being you.

Every time you realize yourself a little more, a deep recognition grows: nothing about you can be discounted. No part of you is a mistake. You are as deliberate as each ray of the sun, individually exquisite, yet as brilliant as the whole. Nothing can be more humbling and invigorating than to realize that your life force is the collective life force, your breath the collective breath, and your heartbeat the rhythm of life.

You're never unplugged. You can only un-realize your connection.

*

You learn to love yourself by being you. That means engaging with the world authentically, every moment of the day. Every thought is a golden opportunity to cultivate greater self-love. You're either loving yourself more or loving yourself less.

As you establish your own source of love within, it takes the pressure off the people around you. You no longer need them to love you a certain way to make you feel whole. Instead, the love you feel for yourself is so abundant, so overflowing, that you gladly share it with others without expecting anything in return. What's more, you're free to receive love any which way it shows up.

It becomes clear that there are no limits on how much love can flow to you and from you, that there is no shortage of love in the world, that everlasting love is an inner state, and that no one stands in the way of you loving yourself more but you.

When you love yourself, you love life.

✳

Self-love knows no conditions and knows no end. It's the love you long for as a child, and the love you hope for as an adult. It's the love you look for in everything you do.

Looking for love from others is where it starts. Finding it in yourself is where it ends. That special someone you dream of meeting, who loves you so deeply, so fully, so unconditionally, is not your partner, not your children, not your parents, not your best friend. The love of your life is not another person. The love of your life is *you*.

CHANGE

Your relationship with change is a mixed bag. You yell, kick, and scream when change means losing something you like. But you roll out the red carpet and welcome it with open arms when it means gaining something you want. You're either deathly afraid of change or can't wait for it to happen.

The times you cannot stand change is when it throws a monkey wrench into your plans. The essence of change flies in the face of the essence of planning, which is to try and prevent the possibility of unwanted things happening. But change isn't just a possibility. It's a promise. Life is a continuous stream of things coming and going. Nothing ever reaches a final state. There are no outcomes you can reliably predict.

There are no outcomes, period.

But when you're in your headspace, you think there are. Outcomes are all you think about. It's all about doing A to get to B to get to C.

The more you steer, the more you get emotionally invested in the goal, the more challenging it becomes to deal with change. It always seems to come at the worst time, which is *any* time as far as your plans are concerned. To the controlling mind, things are *going wrong*.

Ironically, the more detailed your plan is, the more potential there is for something to go wrong. It's no wonder then that you resist change like the plague. You want a guarantee of happiness. But the only guarantee is that change is sure to come.

✳

Actually, change never comes. It's always already here. It's always happening. You can't say *something has changed*. You can only say *something is changing*. Life is never in a static place, and then along comes change. Everything is expanding, contracting, evolving, adapting, collapsing, releasing, reshaping, reforming, restarting. Everything is coming and going. Of course, your mind thinks of it as life interfering with your plans. But you've got it backward.

Life isn't interfering with your plans. Your plans are interfering with life.

✳

As much as you love control, without mystery, your life feels stale and uninspired. When life gets too predictable, everything feels the same, and you're the first in line to invite change. Consciously or unconsciously, you're always the driving force behind your expansion.

Compare yourself to a year ago. Think of all the lessons you've learned since then. Or last week. Or this morning. You're always learning new things about yourself. Even when it feels like you're stuck in a rut, the pressure and boredom of being stuck in a rut builds up and eventually catapults you forward. It's one of the most basic patterns of life: Periods of *less* noticeable growth fuel periods of *very* noticeable growth. Feeling stagnant eventually gives rise to greater focus and determination than before.

If you try to keep conditions from changing, you're in resistance to your own evolution.

✳

Of course, as much as it behooves you to embrace change, it's far easier said than done. Change is inherently difficult. You're being asked to let go of beliefs that are part of your identity, stability, and filtered reality. That's why life has to give you a push. You wouldn't come out of your comfort zones if it didn't.

The more stuck your beliefs are, the harder life pushes you to let them go. Remember, life mirrors your degree of stuckness. It may take severe disturbances to get you to surrender your deepest held beliefs. When this happens, it can be a tumultuous and disconcerting time. It feels like your world is falling apart. But it's only the world of your judgments that's crumbling, the world of *right and wrong*.

Whenever old beliefs fall away, it can prompt any number of emotional and physical symptoms. Sleep issues, exhaustion, confusion, depression, anxiety, and all kinds of aches and pains - the list is endless. Make sure to rule out any physical illness, but always consider the possibility that what you're experiencing is simply growing pains.

During these big shifts, it's essential to give yourself an extra big dose of self-love. Your mind desperately wants to understand what is happening, but there is no precedent for it to find refuge in. It feels like the rug is being pulled out from underneath your life, because to the mind, it is. Suddenly, many of the things you believe are no longer valid. All you can do is give yourself permission to fall apart, and let your new self take hold.

Whenever you're in the throes of change, it's vital to resist muting your senses. Staying in touch with your senses is what keeps you sane. Drugs and intoxicants only interfere with your natural unfolding.

Trust your body's intelligence to sort itself out.

No doubt, it's scary when your inner world changes because the outer world changes with it. You find yourself seeking new relationships, new friendships, new interests, new work. You see things differently and respond differently. Indeed, your whole perspective on life can shift. This re-aligning of the external world with your newfound inner truth can be all-consuming. But as stressful as watching your life reorganize itself can be, there's nothing to fear. Remember, life is a mirror. You only ever manifest that which you're ready for.

Deep down, you're the one creating the change.

✳

Never forget, you're an expansive being. The moment you stop expanding, you become indifferent and bored. Even if you prefer a more predictable life, there needs to be room for change. Otherwise, your soul withers and dies. Even the last earthworm is looking to do something, get somewhere, be who it's meant to be. You can't realize yourself by staying the same. That's just not how life works.

The more you are you, the less you feel threatened by change. You no longer want your life to stay the same. You want it to flow. You embrace continuous transformation as the very essence of life. And you've internalized that for the world to change for the better, you're required to realize yourself more. Be you and be the change.

FEAR

It shouldn't come as a surprise that all fear comes from not being you. When you're in your headspace, confused about who you are, questioning your decisions, trying to please outside voices, and living for outcomes, it's no wonder that there's an undercurrent of fear in everything you do. You fear not getting the things you want because your future happiness depends on them. You fear losing the belongings you've attached your self-worth to. You fear abandonment by the people you rely on to feel loved. And above all, you fear the things that *could* happen.

You might not take a chance because you could fail. You might stay in a mediocre relationship because starting over could be worse. You might pass up an opportunity because you could be successful. As long as you're in your headspace, you can learn to fear anything and everything.

Indeed, what you fear is often the complete opposite of your actual circumstances. You fear being lonely, even though you're in a relationship. You fear not having things, even though you have them. You fear not getting it all done, despite having achieved so much. You fear death, even though you're alive. You can even fear getting healthy because being sick has become part of your identity. Most fears are not about what is in front of you, but what you imagine in your mind.

The rational mind is a master of irrational fears.

Some people even fear the journey of self-realization. They would rather not peel back the layers of stuck feelings for fear of what they might find. Of course, you can't keep a lid on your evolution forever. You're bound to look in the mirror sooner or later.

Even if you don't take a proactive approach to self-realization, eventually, life gives you the necessary push, and all your stuff comes bubbling up. You cannot escape your fears. You must confront them at some point, or else the accumulated suffering becomes unbearable. Fears are the most rigid stuck feelings that keep you out of the flow and separate from your naturally fearless state.

Most of your journey consists of facing your fears.

✳

Ultimately, fear is just like any other emotion. No matter how deep-seated a fear may be, you can learn to release it by observing your sensations. That said, if you've been pushing away certain fears for a long time, perhaps since childhood, they may run so deep that bringing them to the surface can be overwhelming. Should this be the case, don't hesitate to seek support from a mental health professional. A wide range of inspiring and cost-effective therapies continues to evolve. Keep exploring options until you find what works for you. Most important is that you take charge of your emotional well-being and that you no longer feel like a victim.

*

As liberating and healing as it is to release existing fears, it's equally important to keep from developing new ones. The most effective way to prevent new fears from cropping up is to be you. When you listen to your inner voice, there is no opportunity for fear to slip in. You see circumstances as they are and move forward by taking clear action. You know what's true for you and don't feel threatened by the truth of others. You're not lost in regrets about yesterday and have no doubts about what tomorrow may bring. You know, as long as you're being you, there is nothing to fear. You're in the best hands possible.

ATTACHMENT

You know you're attached when your environment dictates how you feel. When things are working in your favor, you're happy. When they're not, you're sad. When others validate you, you gain confidence. When they criticize you, you become insecure. When you're shown affection, you feel loved. When it is withheld, you feel abandoned. As long as you're attached to the world around you, your life is an endless roller coaster of ups and downs.

You can become attached to anything: people, places, pets, your job, your looks, a memory, things you own - and of course, your life. But the biggest attachment of all is to outcomes.

Everything you do from your headspace is with a specific outcome in mind. In fact, you always start with the outcome and then work your way backward, creating a plan for what you think you need to do to get there. This is how you wind up living for the future, disconnected from the now. You no longer do things for the joy of doing them. You do them because of what you expect in return.

Your attachment to outcome can run so deep, you're willing to endure hardship now, so later can be better. You work overtime so you can retire early. You have children so they can take care of you when you're old. You put off pursuing dreams because you would rather play it safe. Essentially, dreams are outcomes you don't trust yourself to pursue because your mind can't conceive of a plan of how to get there. You never stop to consider that anything the mind comes up with is limited to its beliefs and has nothing to do with what's actually possible.

So you continue to chase goals you believe you can achieve, mainly because society says so. Your whole life becomes about living for outcomes, and you completely forget that at the root of all attachments are stuck feelings you can learn to release right now.

Every external goal you're attached to is connected to stuck feelings inside.

*

What makes attachments so tricky is that they start small and grow silently. Over time, even brief interactions with people, places, and things accumulate, and you start to cling to how they make you feel. By the time you realize you're attached, your emotional investment is significant. Severing the attachment at this point means real stress and tangible pain. It can dissuade you from removing yourself from an unhealthy situation, even though your inner voice is telling you to get out. To the mind, a slow trickle of toxicity is more tolerable than cutting the cord to what is known and familiar. But the more feelings get stuck, the more toxicity builds up, and eventually, the situation implodes. You wind up looking back and blaming yourself for not seeing the signs sooner.

But as always, any blame is misplaced. Recognize that everything happens as a reflection of you. Stuck feelings continuously manifest the next set of circumstances that show you how you can realize yourself more.

＊

One of the main milestones in your healing journey is to detach from the world dictating how you feel. Being detached doesn't mean you no longer care or invest your emotions in people, places, and things. It doesn't mean you don't feel sad when you experience loss. It means you no longer need the world to make you happy. You become the source of your own happiness, your own confidence, your own abundance, your own love.

Once you are the source for how you feel, you no longer give to receive. You give freely and receive freely. You get to enjoy a non-controlling, free-to-be-you kind of intimacy with others. You might call it *healthy* attachment, but what really defines your connection is an *absence* of attachment.

In the absence of attachment, love is free to flow.

*

Every thought you believe, every feeling you cling to, is an attachment that interrupts the flow and creates resistance to seeing circumstances as they are. Dissolving your truth structure, the sum total of all your beliefs, is what your journey of self-realization is all about.

Shift from clinging and resisting to allowing, from attaching and controlling to flowing. Be curious and stay open to what each moment brings. Embrace the experience of things coming and going, for the moment you detach, the moment you let go, you become free to be you.

HEALING

There's no question that difficult experiences can affect you deeply. Fears and traumas can torment you and become life-defining battles. Often, all you want is to manage your pain so you can become operational again. Rarely, if at all, do you expect to be as flawless as before.

But as you become more aware of your thoughts, as you experience stuck feelings dissolve, you realize there are no unhealable wounds, there are no permanent scars, there is no everlasting damage. There are only layers of stuck feelings that you can learn to release. The more you release, the more you experience what is underneath: your unhurt, unblemished, unimpaired, fully realized self.

True healing isn't just possible, it's inevitable.

✳

When you experience difficult feelings, it's more important to release them quickly, than to try to understand the root cause. Mental analysis is of secondary importance. The primary objective is to come out of reactivity first. Only then can you see the situation for what it is, take clear action, and make positive changes so unhealthy situations don't repeat. But if don't come out of reactivity, you can't hear your inner voice, and resistance and confrontation ensue.

＊

The more you heal yourself, the more your healing capacity grows beyond yourself. Your mere presence is soothing to everyone around you. Your attention, compassion, and listening skills help others let go of their stuck feelings. You find yourself taking on the unresolved pain of your lineage, your gender, your generation, your era. At first, you might resist the calling to heal wounds that aren't yours. But that's how powerful you are. As you heal yourself, you have no choice but to become a healer.

By healing yourself, you heal the world.

＊

Once you release stuck feelings, they are no longer part of your filtered reality. A brand new life experience opens up. Indifference turns into inspiration. Scarcity turns into abundance. Limitations turn into beauty. Fears give way to the endless possibilities and uninhibited creativity of life.

Healing allows life to flow and being in the flow is your natural state. Instead of living for outcomes, live for the simplicity of the incoming moment. Instead of seeking love on the outside, find it within. Instead of trying to make life happen, let it happen. Instead of figuring it out in advance, figure yourself out as you go.

Life is an unrelenting force that never gives up on you. Everything is designed to help you realize how perfect you already are. You cannot avoid it.

You are meant to heal.

HAPPINESS

From the moment you open your eyes, you become conditioned to look for happiness in the world around you. It's easy to see why. The world is full of allure. There is no end to the glamorous images that present themselves. You get pulled into the persuasion that happiness is found in work, money, power, relationships, food, sex, drugs, shopping, entertainment. Without knowing it, you become firmly committed to the idea that happiness is some combination of those things.

But the moment you achieve anything, the joy from achieving it starts to fade, the old dissatisfaction returns, and you feel no happier than before. That assumes you even reach your goal. More often, change interferes with your plans, you get discouraged, and your fickle mind jumps to something else. The years go by, and you start to worry that you might never find true happiness. Welcome to the roller coaster of living in your headspace. You keep making plans and pursuing outcomes because your mind believes you need to plan for your future happiness. It doesn't realize that planning is what gets in the way of you being happy now.

To the mind, planning for your future happiness makes perfect sense. It seems so simple. All you have to do is get rid of the things you don't like and keep the things you do. Sounds easy enough! Just execute your plan, hit your milestones, and when only the positives remain, you've made it. You've earned your happiness.

Of course, things always turn out differently. Try as you might, the lasting happiness you yearn for continues to elude you. You don't understand why. Looking around, everyone else seems to be happy, seems to have figured it out. Why can't you be just as happy? Doubt and fear start to creep in that you're doing something wrong, that you might never get to that happy place, that all your efforts are in vain, that everyone else gets to live a happy life, but you.

All of this anxiety comes from your mind attaching happiness to outcomes. *If you achieve this, it makes you happy. If you buy that, it brings you joy.* You see others showing off stuff and assume they are happy because of it. Your mind never considers the social masks people wear to make themselves look happy and successful. Instead, your mind correlates owning stuff with being happy. So you put more pressure on yourself to steer harder, think smarter, move faster. You tell yourself to analyze more precisely, research more thoroughly, choose more decidedly, act with greater determination, acquire more expertise, summon more willpower, improve your timing, and work your fingers to the bone. Because, according to your plans, you should be happy by now. And if you're not, it means you're not trying hard enough, or you're doing everything wrong.

But you're not doing everything wrong. The issue is not that the things you want can't make you happy. They can! The issues arise from expecting those things to make you *permanently* happy.

There are many things in life that make you jump up and down with unbridled joy. There are big occasions, like graduations, promotions, the birth of a child, or achieving a personal best. And there are little, everyday nuances that bring a smile to your face, like an unexpected compliment from a stranger or a parking spot opening up, right when you get there. All of those things can bring you happiness. The key is to recognize it's only *temporary* happiness. Just like the things themselves come and go, so does the happiness they bring.

All feelings you encounter in life are as impermanent as life itself.

✷

The notion that nothing is permanent is the hardest concept for the mind to grasp. It works hard day and night to make things permanent, controllable, and known. Acknowledging that nothing lasts forever goes against its very nature. To the mind, unpredictability is a *bad* thing.

Yet, once you come out of your headspace, and connect with the flow of things coming and going, you realize the unknown is a *beautiful* thing. There is so much more in store for you than the stale repository of what you already know. Every unknown moment brings with it the endless possibilities of life's flow, eager to enter your field of experiences.

But you block that flow by clinging to feelings that make you happy, for fear that losing them will make you unhappy. Instead of being open to new feelings, you dwell on the memory of old ones. Instead of finding joy in the continuity of things coming and going, you seek lasting joy in the things themselves.

As a result of all this clinging, your inner voice grows distant, and you rely on outside voices telling you that true happiness must be earned and that your best days are yet to come. But seeking your future happiness is the surest way to diminish the quality of your life right now. And right now is the only experience that's real.

If you wait for your happy future to arrive, you continue to be unhappy because you're aligned with the expectation that tomorrow is always better.

＊

Chasing your happiness never gets easier. It only gets harder. Not only does the world around you keep changing, your ideas of what constitutes happiness also don't stay the same. Your mind is always re-analyzing, re-formulating, re-assessing your plans, abandoning some of them or all of them, and coming up with new ones. It can never stay focused on one thing long enough because it's too fickle to wait for the results. Without immediate validation, doubts start to creep in. You might still be at the drawing board of one idea when your mind decides that the current approach isn't working and that a better plan is needed.

But every time you redefine your vision of happiness, it kills any momentum from before. You feel the day when suffering ends and happiness begins is farther away than ever. When both the world and your opinions of it are constantly changing, it's no wonder you get tired of projecting what you think makes you happy, onto a version of yourself you have yet to become, under circumstances that have yet to occur, in a future that you cannot predict, all the while sacrificing the things that bring you joy now. With so much noise in your headspace, why wouldn't you feel empty, exhausted, and disillusioned?

Planning for your future happiness is a kind of madness.

✳

The good news is, with so much trial and error, somewhere along the way it dawns on you that permanent happiness doesn't come from the things around you. Those things are meant to come and go. But the one thing that *is* permanent in your experience of life is *you*. True happiness comes from being you. And you can only be you *now*.

Life is designed to make you happy by showing you all the ways you make yourself unhappy. The world keeps mirroring your limitations until you recognize your limitlessness. Your job is to stay open to receiving, unrestricted in giving, exhilarated about being, and excited to find out what comes next.

Cooperate with life and let the joy of flowing with it unfold. A deep sense of happiness emerges from within that cannot be taken away, no matter what situations arise. Ultimately, circumstances don't bring you happiness. You bring your happiness to circumstances.

PURPOSE

You can have all the comfort and prestige in the world. Without purpose, your life feels dull, empty, meaningless. It feels like the most important piece is missing.

Growing up, family expectations, education systems, career ladders, and social norms shape and even determine your understanding of your purpose. Some of those voices are well-meaning, while others blindly perpetuate their own programming. But rarely does anyone take the time to ask you how *you* feel? What life do *you* want to live?

It's not that goals other people tell you to pursue can't be fulfilling - they can - but the calling has to come from you. As long as you follow outside voices instead of your inner one, it doesn't matter what you do, you're not being true to yourself, and so your purpose cannot reveal itself.

If you're not listening to your inner voice, you're not living your own life.

*

The longer you ignore your inner voice, the deeper you dig yourself into a hole - the hole of not being you. You can check off all the social expectation boxes you want. Chasing goals that are not your own only leads to dissatisfaction, anxiety, and depression.

An easy way to tell if a goal stems from outside voices is that it's always accompanied by the fear of not reaching it. Remember, mental programming is always focused on the outcome. A goal emanating from your personal truth, however, has the moment-to-moment backing of your inner voice. Sure, you may have a sense of the direction you're going, but your primary focus is on how you feel right now. As a result, you don't carry a specific-enough picture of the future for you to get upset about not reaching.

Take this simple test: Think of an important life goal you have - something you really want to achieve. Now imagine not achieving it. Assess honestly: Is the thought of not achieving it unbearable? Do you refuse to consider a future that is any different? Does the idea of not getting to live the life you imagine bring up fear and anxiety? If so, this attachment to outcome indicates that your goal might not be your own. If that is the case, a thorough and honest reassessment might be in order, of discovering your inner truth and aligning your outer circumstances.

*

Even if you're not listening to the voices of others, even if you feel like your actions are serving your own needs, there is an even deeper, more intricate reason you might be focused on certain outcomes. And that is to cover up internal lack.

Very often, the whole picture of what you want from life, all the outcomes you hope to achieve, is a reflection of something you're missing inside. You then set your sights on achieving those things in the hope they give you what you're missing. For example, lack of self-love motivates you to look for affection in relationships. Lack of abundance compels you to accumulate possessions. Lack of confidence has you seeking power and social prestige. Look at your life, closely and honestly, and see if any external goals point to internal lack.

Always start from within and build outwards.

Releasing all those stuck feelings isn't just essential for your well-being. It has a direct impact on you discovering your outer purpose. The more you release stuck feelings, the less you feel the need to steer to achieve certain outcomes, and the more you open yourself up to receiving. You can tell when this is happening because life gets easier. Good things come to you without even trying. An ocean of confidence and energy arises from within. It feels so good and so right to be you, you're not even thinking about tomorrow. Yet, you don't doubt for a second that wherever you're going is where you're supposed to be going.

*

Goals that arise from your inner voice don't start with the outcome and then have you working towards it. Instead, your future reveals itself, one authentic moment at a time, until the bigger picture comes into focus. Remember, you're on a journey. Life is continuously unfolding. As long as you listen, you're always shown the next step.

Once you're comfortable letting life lead the way, you get to enjoy the unfolding without worrying about results because your fulfillment does not depend on achieving them. You're not fearful of what could happen or frustrated about what should be happening. The thought of giving up never crosses your mind because, well, you're not in your mind. When you're following your inner voice, giving up is not an option.

Your deepest fulfillment comes from being in alignment with yourself, every step of the way.

Be grateful and supportive when you see others who are genuinely passionate about what they're doing. Let the essence of their alignment inspire you. It doesn't matter if what they're doing agrees with you or not. Agreeing is judgment, and judgment shuts down the flow. Your role in life is to support the flow. Taking part in another person's joy is to honor the way of the world. Celebrate when others generate the energy of alignment in themselves, for the energy of alignment is contagious. That's what you're all working towards, anyway.

*

Watching your external purpose manifest from your inner alignment is the ultimate adventure. It may show up as a single lifetime calling or many different chapters. Whether you impact many lives or just a few, whether you fly under the radar or make headlines - external acclaim plays no role in being you. You are not defined by what you do, anyway. You are always you, doing things.

Should you feel like you haven't been living your purpose, don't despair. Every leg of your journey plays a part in your evolution. All insights build on the experiences you have gathered, and all experiences are a reflection of you. *This* is just a continuation of *that*. Stay connected to your inner voice and keep building a life of greater alignment with your true self. To that end, ask yourself:

What does being you look like right now?

*

Remember, you cannot fail. Your inner voice is here to guide you every step of the way. As you become more of you, the world around you reflects your becoming. Live freely, and let go freely. There is always more life to be lived. Your purpose, always and forever, is to be you.

TRUTH

Have you ever wondered why everyone seems to have a different truth? And why others disagreeing with yours is your greatest source of irritation? It can keep you up all night, consumed by thoughts of how to convince the other side, and how to save them from their ignorance. After all, you're one hundred percent certain that you are right and they are wrong.

The more obvious you think the truth is, the more your frustration builds. You waver between the exhilaration of your heartfelt conviction and the disbelief that others don't see it your way. At first, you tread softly. *How can I get them to agree with me?* But quickly you feel like strangling them. *How can they be so stupid? Why don't they get it?* You try to reference others who think like you, to make it look like you're in the majority. Then being right becomes being normal, and being normal means being right.

Of course, the other side never comes around because they want to convince you *they're* right. Arguments and counter-arguments ensue. Everyone is out to prove they're right, under the guise of creating a better world.

But underneath it all, it's not about creating a better world. It's not even about being right. It's about avoiding the unknown. Sound familiar? What you consider true and false is your mind attempting to project the known onto the unknown, and the more others share your projections, the better you feel about them.

Everyone has different truths because they filter reality differently.

*

But it gets even more convoluted. As much as you want to convince others that you're right and they're wrong, deep down, you don't actually want everyone else to agree with you. If everyone agreed with you, there would be no one to make wrong. You need someone to be wrong for you to be right. Otherwise, you have to find a new mission. For the mind, creating circumstances that enable it to be right is a purpose in and of itself.

Showing off your rightness can be expressed in many ways. You might claim your approach is better by pointing to things that have worked in the past. You might quote an authority figure in the space, defending their perspective as if it were your own. Or you insist on being right, simply because you're better, louder, or more forceful at arguing.

One of the most popular ways to argue for your truth is by using a special category of labels, called *facts*. In a mind-based world, facts represent the ultimate truth. Having facts on your side is your ticket to credibility. It's a social confirmation of your rightness. You use facts from scientific studies, group consensus, or historical data to bolster your case for why the world would be a better place if everyone came to the light. *Your* light.

In all of this back and forth, everyone thinks they're arguing for the truth. But arguing for something is never about the truth. It's always about being right, and at a deeper level about covering up the unknown. History is littered with wars over who's more right than the other.

✳

Every truth you identify with creates resistance to the flow of life. When you declare one thing right, you implicitly make all other possibilities wrong. When you agree with one thing, you disagree with everything else.

The effort of maintaining your truths is enormous. Every piece of information you encounter is a potential new truth that must be evaluated against your existing ones. Individual truths become entangled and uphold each other, to create an increasingly complex structure of interdependent truths. This *truth structure* is constantly under attack. Every headline you hear, or conversation you have, threatens the stability of everything you believe in. When you encounter new inputs, you can't be at peace until you've processed and negotiated, with yourself and others, so that all your truths are once again neatly tucked away in a cohesive pattern that makes rational sense.

Of course, as long as you're in your headspace, you're not aware that any of this is happening because processing and negotiating is how your mind works. But the more you practice thought awareness, the more you sense that your mind is always on the edge of doubt and fear that your truths may no longer be valid.

To reduce the anxiety of possibly finding out that you're wrong, your mind instinctively shields itself from potential new truths by blocking out new information. You can observe this *confirmation bias* in yourself. Whenever you seek out new information, you're inclined to look for that which you already agree with. In your environment, it's likely you primarily associate with people whose views mirror your own. It's rare that someone you disagree with is also your friend. Especially later in life, when belief structures become exceedingly dense and change-averse, it becomes nearly impossible for people to accept new truths.

It's much easier to surround yourself with existing truths than to explore new ones.

But surrounding yourself with only the like-minded comes with its own stressors. The pressure of *groupthink* is immense. The group's beliefs are its bond, so new ideas are a threat. Should any member of the group dare to question the prevailing narrative, they are quickly ridiculed, marginalized, and even expelled.

Groupthink can happen in your family, circle of friends, and at the broadest socio-economic and political levels. From backyard water cooler conversations to presidential elections, everywhere people are arguing with each other in the name of one truth versus the other. The winning side gets to parade their truth around as being *more* true than the losing side's truth. Clearly, the winner's truth must be the right one, since it has enabled them to fight a better fight. The losing parties whimper off, reeling from their shattered beliefs. But it doesn't take long for them to regroup and set out to prove to the world once again that their truth is ultimately the right one. Of course, when everyone thinks they are righteous, unrighteous things happen.

Bringing change to groupthink is slow and difficult. The more tight-knit the group, the harder it is for individual members to explore and discover their inner voice. Group activities monopolize everyone's time and energy and suffocate the innate desire for self-realization. Dysfunctional patterns are perpetuated and can become even more pronounced because of the collective resistance to letting in new energy. The group's dynamic becomes stagnant and repetitive. This is how families, social groups, communities, and nations continue acting out blind beliefs and behaviors for generation after generation. Everyone keeps doing things the way they've been doing them - for no other reason than that's how they've been doing them.

✳

Ultimately, your truths are your greatest limitations. Remember, you don't just label a few things as true or false. Your mind labels *everything* it encounters. A cloud can't float by without you forming an opinion of it. The sun can't set without your mental commentary. The moment you identify something by calling it a name, you've already judged it.

As you walk through life, you become increasingly opinionated. Only the things you consider to be true get your attention. Everything else is devalued. It becomes essential to defend your truths to uphold your filtered reality. What you don't realize is that constant judging takes you out of the flow. You're no longer in receiving mode. Instead of casting the widest net possible, your opinions limit you to what you think is possible.

Truth derived from your headspace can never account for the immense complexity and diversity, let alone the paradoxes of life. At the end of the day, your truth structure is little more than a neatly packaged set of beliefs you hold onto until life forces you to let them go. Then your life falls apart until you assemble a new set of beliefs, and then you cling to those until the next breakdown. Fortunately, with each restart your beliefs become simpler and less absolute. Slowly, but surely, that seemingly unwavering truth structure dissolves.

The more inalienable you believe your truths to be, the more life challenges you to let them go.

Of course, experiencing breakdown after breakdown is a hard way to live. But this is what your mind does to you. You have to crash and burn before you let go of your beliefs. Your life falls apart, over and over again.

The good news is your life doesn't have to fall apart. You don't need to experience truth crisis after truth crisis. You can learn to live in the flow of new moments coming and going. You have a set of tools now to come out of the reactivity of your mind. By practicing thought awareness, releasing stuck feelings, and taking clear action, you start to expand beyond the world of your self-limiting beliefs. With your thoughts out of the way, life is free to flow, and your true self is free to lead the way.

KNOWLEDGE

Until you label a tree *a tree*, it is just something that exists. You're aware of it. You can see it. You can feel its presence. But you haven't yet created a definition in your head. And because your mind isn't consumed by trying to explain what you're perceiving, you get to relax. You get to stay in your body and experience the sensation of just being.

The relief from staying out of your headspace is real, tangible, and instantly restorative. The immense pressure from all that mental noise, from your mind's incessant need for knowing and controlling, is absent. This gives way to an even deeper experience of life, one marked by curiosity, awe, and wonder.

You get a glimpse of this state of awe in moments of spontaneity when you're swept away by the excitement of doing something without much planning or time for anticipation. It's exciting because you haven't burdened yourself with thoughts and expectations. Instead, you're tapped into the flow of things coming and going, and you coming and going with things. The mind, of course rejects this behavior, it thinks there is no order. But to be in the flow is not about rules. It's to live without limitations.

Nothing is more magical and exhilarating than being plugged in to all that is possible.

The moment you label the tree *a tree*, however, you get pulled into your headspace. Your mind takes over and your mental reactivity flares up. Definitions, explanations, and past experiences rush in and interrupt the pure experience of being with the tree, and the tree being with you.

Something very precious gets lost the moment you think you know something. Life is no longer about endless abundance entering and exiting your experience. Instead, it's all about your mind's desperate obsession with turning the unknown into the known. And everything that becomes known loses its mystery. That's why living life through your headspace becomes drab and dull. All you see is the limited number of static objects you've defined in your previous experiences. Think of how many trees you walk past every day. You barely notice them, if at all. Even when you look at one, you don't see its aliveness. You don't see how fresh and unique every aspect of it is, how every branch twists and turns differently, how every leaf has life's boundless creativity flowing through it. No two trees are alike, even when they're the same kind. Yet, when you're in your head and you look at any one of them, all you see is *a tree*.

All the breathtaking detail of life is lost once you think you know something. Instead of experiencing the miracle of life, you experience the definitions in your head.

✳

That doesn't mean knowledge is useless - far from it. You wouldn't be able to function without knowing things. You need knowledge to formulate strategies, execute tasks, and improve skills. Figuring out how stuff works can provide the biggest thrill and help you achieve excellence in your craft. A moment of insight is a moment of awe and wonder that can inspire you to a lifetime of greatness.

Knowledge can foster a deep passion and reverence for life by highlighting the ingenious order and impossible complexity underlying all things in existence. It can even point to the possibility of things yet to come. The deeper your understanding of life, the more profound your experience of it can be - but only as long as knowledge doesn't become truth unto itself.

Comprehending the characteristics of a particular molecule can be compelling. But appreciating how it has come to have those characteristics is beyond comprehension.

✳

You would think the most knowledgeable persons are also the most awe-inspired ones. But that's not necessarily the case. Knowledge can keep you deeply mired in your headspace. It can literally go to your head. From there, what you know becomes truth, while the backdrop to why things are even knowable is lost. Without this backdrop, what you know is accountable only to itself. And this is where living in your head can be dangerous. Intellect alone can justify any behavior, any action, any outcome. It has no conscience. Only when knowledge serves as a reminder of the miracle of life has it fulfilled its purpose.

In a world obsessed with evidence, however, you are not taught to honor that miracle. You are taught to obey your mind.

You are told to think of knowledge as truth, not as a means to hold space for the unknowable.

As you traverse through the institutions of modern life, you are required to know more and more. Your connection to the open-minded wonder of *not knowing* fades, and acquiring greater knowledge and expertise becomes the primary focus of your existence. You are pushed to become a master of knowing, while lack of knowledge is associated with shame, guilt, and weakness. You can observe this in yourself. Whenever you come across something you don't know, notice the urge to look it up, including everybody else's opinion of it.

✳

In a society where knowledge is king, the more details you know about something, the greater your position of power. Every day, whether you're aware of it or not, you use your knowledge to judge others for not knowing or knowing differently, just so you can feel right and in control.

But it's a fleeting sense of right and a desperate sense of control. Deep down, you're aware that all knowledge fades. You either forget because you can't retain every detail, or it becomes naturally obsolete. Few so-called facts survive intact for more than a few generations. Sooner or later, they are supplanted by the next generation's efforts to use facts to tell *their* stories, to give *their* lives structure and meaning.

Ultimately, all facts are created by humans using their minds. And the only thing a human mind can produce is an opinion in the context of a story. Everyone uses facts to tell the story they want to promote. Facts support the story, not the other way around.

✻

Just like all things in life come and go, so should your knowledge of those things. No doubt, understanding the physical world is a beautiful thing, and it contributes to experiencing it fully. But issues arise when you refuse to let go of your knowledge, or worse, rely on it for your identity and purpose. It's like putting your faith in a sandcastle that the tide keeps washing away. Life is fluid. Your knowledge should be, too.

True peace of mind cannot come from clinging to what you know. It comes from letting it go.

✳

Enjoy knowledge as it informs the depth and breadth of your three-dimensional world. But let it go just as willingly, so you can experience every moment unfolding anew. Then it becomes possible for you to be with the tree and experience it without needing to label it. And it becomes possible for the tree to be with you because you're no longer keeping yourself separate from it.

To be in the flow is to experience life without labels. Let any fear of what might come, give way to the fascination of seeing what happens next. Live not in the temporary knowledge of things, but the unknowable miracle of life passing through.

CHOICE

Few things can light up your headspace as choice can. That's because to the mind choice means control. The more options you have, so the thinking goes, the more likely you are to pick the one that's right for you.

But choice is entirely a mental concept. It pulls you into your headspace, where *right* and *wrong* dictate how you navigate a particular situation. To arrive at the conclusion of *right,* you must go through the entire process of ruling out what's *wrong.* That means analyzing, evaluating, comparing, revisiting, and sleeping over anything you find. Your mind is firmly in the driver's seat, on a mission to achieving the outcome of absolute certainty.

At first, you don't see the issue with that. After all, you want to be sure you're making the right decisions. You may even get a thrill from all the options. The idea of being in control of your destiny is mesmerizing. You want to be the captain of your ship, the grandmaster of your life's fortunes. More options mean more possibilities to control your fate.

But quickly, the thrill of having so many options fades, and a different reality sets in. One moment one particular choice seems to be *the one*, the next moment another. You can be utterly convinced you've made the right decision stepping into the shower and not even remember it when you get out.

But don't feel bad. It's that fickle mind at work again. It's actually doing an excellent job, given that it's designed to compare facts and figures, and analyze data points. But when you ask it to tap into a deeper wisdom and choose what's in alignment with *you,* it stutters and fails.

Your mind doesn't know you. It's just a tool you use.

✳

In fact, the more choices you have, the *less* likely you are to make a decision. You keep weighing your options, connecting the dots one way, then another way, introducing new possibilities, and modifying old ones. All too often, the decision you wind up making is not the one you believe is the best. It's the one you settle on because you've exhausted yourself thinking about it. And when you do finally make a choice, you've become so overly invested in the outcome that nothing can live up to your expectations. Disappointment is virtually a guarantee.

Of course, there are instances when you *are* happy with a choice you've made. But alas, the next situation is already waiting for you with a new set of options. Not only do you have little time to enjoy the fruits of a good decision, but new choices can cast previous decisions in a different light, potentially turning old good choices into new bad ones.

This choice loop is a maddening affair. It always starts out so promising and invigorating. All your hopes and desires perk up. But once your analytical mind kicks in, the situation inevitably turns into a train wreck. You wind up frustrated and spent when all you've wanted is to choose something that makes you happy. But you never get there because the choosing process itself makes you unhappy.

✳

It's an arduous road forward to keep looking for the best choice. Whenever you think you've found one, there's a nagging doubt about whether it really is. That's because living in your headspace means living in constant comparison. A part of you is always looking for something better. This feeling of inconclusiveness and uncertainty wears you down. Your mind says you're not doing a good job navigating life, that you need to choose better. But this is a self-sustaining fallacy. The goal is never to learn to choose better.

The goal is to recognize your mind is not the right tool for choosing what's aligned with you.

The good news is you don't need to choose your way through life. You don't have to weigh every option and anticipate every outcome. All you have to do is listen to your inner voice. All you have to do is be you now. Every time you choose to be you, another pebble gets added to your path, and the bigger picture reveals itself. This is where infinite trust and confidence arise. You know your future is the brightest future possible because being you is what takes you there.

Ultimately, choosing not to be you isn't a choice. Life wants you to be you. Everything you experience points you *toward* your fully realized self, never away from it. To choose not to be you only delays the inevitable. You are meant to be you. You already are.

TRUST

Trust generated by the mind is always based on conditions. As long as your conditions are met, you continue trusting. If they're no longer met, you stop trusting. Trust is a feeling your mind generates in response to feeling in control.

What's so tricky about it, is that while you're feeling it, it couldn't be more real. But conditional trust always comes with an undercurrent of anxiety and tension. At some level, you're aware that the world is ever-changing; that people, places, and things are ever-evolving; that you are ever-expanding. You can feel how your mind keeps jumping around, assigning importance to random thoughts. When the nature of life is steeped in continuous change, and you base your trust on conditions staying the same, it's hard not to fear that it can evaporate at any time - because it can. From one moment to the next, you can lose trust in a person you've trusted all your life.

*

When it comes to trust, living in your headspace is a double whammy. Not only is it difficult to trust others, but you also lack fundamental trust in yourself. Remember, your mind is constantly comparing your beliefs to the world around you, looking for confirmation of its truth structure. As long as your identity relies on outside validation, you can never really trust yourself, because your mind only trusts what it knows, and all knowledge - whether about yourself or others - is fleeting.

In essence, the mind doesn't know how to trust.

That's what makes life lived through the mental lens such a roller coaster. Nothing is reliable. That's because nothing is supposed to be reliable, at least not in the way the mind needs it to be. The mind's notion of trust requires life to stand still. It requires incoming circumstances to match your previously imagined ones. And that's just not how life works.

*

Living in your head cuts you off from your inner voice. Any trust you generate is part of your mind's ongoing knowing-and-controlling efforts, keeping you singularly focused on the world around you, not the world within you.

But when you're connected to your body, in touch with your sensations, you respond to circumstances exactly as they are. You don't need trust to make up for anything that isn't there. Everything real is already there. And you're not wasting time and energy reacting to things that aren't. Ultimately, expectations are nothing but distractions from experiencing your circumstances as they show up.

That doesn't mean you shouldn't care when others don't keep their word. Of course, you want them to show up as promised. Of course, it's disappointing if they don't. But as long as you're grounded in your truth, you don't plummet to the depths of despair. Instead, you know how to manage any uncomfortable feelings that arise. Observe them, release them, and take clear action on whether or not you want to move forward with this person in your life.

*

Being you gives rise to a much deeper trust that originates from far beyond your mind's eye. To be grounded in the intentionality of your being is to be connected to the unimaginable collaboration of life forces that have come together as you. It's to feel the calm assurance of flowing with the greater current. It's to be equally as kind and caring to yourself as you are to others. It's to recognize how everything is designed to bring out the very best in you, and that if you trust being you, life takes care of the rest.

VALUES

Have you ever considered why every individual has their own set of values? Why every society and culture espouses a different set of agreed-upon views? Because that's all that values are, views.

Your values are your deepest held beliefs. They are your strongest opinions. They run so deep that you know not where they come from. They are inextricably intertwined with your identity. You cannot imagine yourself without them. They represent your untouchable, unquestionable, undeniable truth. Your moral compass. They are so intimately linked to your sense of *this is who I am* that when someone questions them, it feels like an attack on your integrity, your character, your emotional sanctuary.

At the collective level, shared social norms can be a great bond for the people of a nation. But they can also be the cause of division between people of different origins.

For different cultures to recognize the common humanity they share, each individual must come out of identification with the conditioned beliefs of their environment and find their personal truth within. Inner truth is the only truth that doesn't clash with the truth of others.

World peace is when every person is at peace with themselves.

Until then, differences in values provide ample fodder for judgment, at all levels. If you're honest with yourself, you might discover it in your own behavior. Do you have co-workers who embrace different traditions? Do you have a family member who makes lifestyle choices you would never make? Have you ever ended a relationship over irreconcilable differences? It's easy to say one should respect other people's values. But do you? Do you ever quietly wonder *why are they like that?* Do you ever privately think to yourself *they're weird?* In most cases, *values* are a coverup for judgment. They are socially sanctioned opinions that are often even protected by law.

Even admiring other countries or cultures for *doing it better* is judgment. It's all a reflection of living in a state of comparison, believing in separateness, feeling the need to defend that which you hold as true, unaware that real inner truth never needs external validation.

That doesn't mean you shouldn't enjoy, even uphold, your favorite cultural traditions. Enjoy the heck out of your three-dimensional experience. Just don't cling too hard when the winds of change come blowing.

✳

Ultimately, values arise from stuck feelings, usually inherited from your cultural surroundings, that manifest as conditions you put on yourself and your environment. They are deeply fused with your truth structure and inform much of your filtered reality. To the mind, it feels like adhering to your values keeps you safe and on track with your happy future. But more often than not, values are giant blind spots of ingrained beliefs that perpetuate judgment of others who believe differently. They keep you mired in the dense reactivity of your head, disconnected from your inner voice, limiting the otherwise infinite space you get to realize yourself in.

The more inalienable you think your values are, the more they limit your expansion.

The purest form of living your life is to respond to circumstances as they happen, and take clear action based on what resonates and what doesn't. To deny a situation from unfolding based on preconceived notions of what it should be is to rob yourself of the opportunity to be a co-creator of life.

If you're ever unsure about whether you're picking up a conditioned belief or an inner truth, the easiest way to tell the difference is to look for the presence of fear. Stuck feelings masquerading as values are always accompanied by the fear of having to confront the unknown that lies beneath, primarily, the threat of losing one's identity. *If I*

don't reaffirm my values, then who am I? If I don't follow
my beliefs, then what becomes of me?

In contrast, guidance arising from your inner voice never requires the approval of others, nor does it cast any doubts as to what might happen next. You're simply moving forward in lockstep with the great unfolding of life.

The takeaway is not for you to go and actively try to deny your values from now on. They provide a necessary structure and lens for where you are currently. Remember, you cannot become the person you are meant to be, by denying who you are right now. Just realize that your journey of self-realization is to release yourself from all of your beliefs.

Every belief you cling to interrupts the flow of life. Every belief you release brings you more in sync with it. All thoughts and feelings are meant to come and go. The only thing that is of permanent value is being you.

RELATIONSHIPS

Romantic relationships are one of the great accelerators of self-realization. On the surface, it looks like you're looking for simple compatibility. You want to be with someone who has the qualities you deem attractive, usually consisting of some combination of looks, personality, chemistry, accomplishments, and goals. You think the closer someone matches your picture of the ideal partner, the happier and longer-lasting you can expect the relationship to be. But you rarely stop to examine what has created that picture of your perfect partner in the first place.

As usual, stuck feelings are at the root of it all. Just like you avoid people who trigger you in negative ways, you gravitate towards people who trigger you in positive ways. Everything is about your triggers. And feeling triggered is never about the other person. It's all about you.

It's no surprise then that your top requirement is to be with someone who validates your truth structure, all those beliefs you carry about yourself and the world. Next, you want them to make up for the things you lack inside. Have you ever wondered why you keep attracting the same kind of people with whom you recreate the same dynamics that trigger you in the same ways? It's not happening to annoy you. It's happening because you haven't resolved those particular issues. As long as you carry stuck feelings, you keep manifesting circumstances that point them out to you. That's how life works. That's how you learn to realize yourself more.

You are the instigator of your own evolution.

✳

If you're in a committed relationship, reflect on how stuck feelings may be impacting the way you interact with each other. They express themselves as conditions you bestow upon the relationship. When your conditions are met, you feel confident and secure about your future together. When the conditions aren't met, your love feels threatened. From one moment to the next, someone you think you love can suddenly feel like a stranger or even an enemy.

That's why the so-called honeymoon phase is such an important part of blossoming romance. It's by no means incidental fluff. The initial bliss is an essential part of the bonding experience. It provides the opportunity to establish a baseline - as idealistic as it may be - from which to work through stuck feelings later on. If everyone had to confront each other's stuck feelings right from the start, few relationships would ever get off the ground.

Furthermore, many of the idealistic projections that arise early on are themselves representations of stuck feelings. You can see why new relationships are such an accelerator of personal growth. In record time you become aware of a record number of stuck feelings.

Indeed, once stuck feelings surface, it can be a rude awakening. You might feel disappointed, even deceived, by your partner for not disclosing their true identity from the start. Or you might blame yourself for not seeing the signs sooner. Either way, don't be hard on yourself. You're navigating new territory. You're bringing out different sides in each other. Hence, every new relationship contains an element of surprise, of perceived misrepresentation. You're doing it, too. The thrill of a new person in your life motivates you to be at your best. It comes from a well-intentioned place. And who knows, some of your best might become more permanent because of it.

Ultimately, there's no reason to get upset when your special someone turns out to be different than the person they've projected themselves to be. Not only are a big part of those projections your own, but your partner goes through their own experience of waking up to who you are in the context of their life. Eventually, it all evens out, everyone's behavior normalizes and how you deal with each other's stuck feelings becomes the true test of your mettle.

*

Whatever conditions you put on your relationship, at the root it's always a lack of self-love. Remember, everything you feel like you're missing on the inside, you seek to fulfill from the outside. If you're unkind to yourself, you seek kindness from others. If you're unforgiving towards yourself, you seek forgiveness from others. If you don't love yourself in certain ways, you look for others to love you in precisely those ways.

That doesn't mean there's anything wrong with you. Life is never about right or wrong. Yes, difficult situations happen because you manifest them from stuck feelings. But it's not happening for you to blame yourself. It's happening to give you another chance to heal and move beyond. In fact, stuck feelings only surface when you're ready to let them go. You're always asked to face the next most immediate block on your journey. So when you feel the calling to enter into a relationship, it's because you're ready to experience growing pains in the name of love.

Always look for the lessons contained within your attraction to others. You're attracted for a reason. And those reasons can be both positive and negative triggers, depending on your internal makeup. It is just as possible to be attracted to a caring person, as it is to an abusive one because what you know is often less scary than what you don't. In any case, every trigger is an opportunity to self-reflect, observe your sensations, and release stuck feelings.

*

The holy grail of all relationships is to be with someone who sees you for who you are and doesn't want you to be different. The ideal partner is someone who can hold space for you to fall in love with yourself.

Giving each other the space for self-love is the best possible foundation for falling in love with each other.

Between self-loving individuals, love can flow freely. Everyone can be themselves. You get to be lovers, collaborators, confidants. You get to support each other's causes or work together on a joint mission. You make each other feel seen and heard, and feelings can be shared and let go of again. To truly love each other is to be holders of each other's self-love. Even if you wind up growing apart, your mutual respect and humanity remain intact.

*

If you're currently in a relationship that is experiencing friction, the first thing to look at is whether or not you are giving each other enough physical space. It's important to miss each other sometimes. If you never miss each other, if you're too close, you might be smothering your love. Your passion becomes muted, and you take each other for granted. But if you're too distant, your intimate connection suffers. Finding the right balance is an ongoing effort, but spending time apart is essential for keeping things fresh.

The next thing to look at is whether or not there is enough non-physical space. Meaning, are your energies always intertwined? Do you give each other enough breathing room? Just because you're in the same room together doesn't mean you always need to be interacting. Especially when you live together, it's essential to learn to be together in stillness, doing your own thing. There's something exquisite about two people who are connected while being at peace with themselves.

Lastly, and most importantly, look at all the ways you feel triggered by your partner. Rather than putting it all on them, reflect on those triggers. They point to stuck feelings inside of you, internal knots that need to be dissolved.

It's best to talk about it. You can't tip-toe around each other's stuck feelings for long. If you don't address them when they first show up, it only gets harder as resentment builds. Commit to the task of peeling back the layers, individually, as well as together, and work on releasing stuck feelings, as they give rise to the conditions you put on each other. Only then can self-love blossom - and with it, unconditional love for each other.

The greatest treasure is someone who can hold space for you to fall in love with yourself.

Be mindful of relationships that trigger you constantly. Your partner shouldn't just trigger you, they should also give you the space to reflect, release, and come out of it. If you don't feel safe, if there's not enough quiet time, then there isn't enough breathing room for you to heal and grow. Assess honestly whether this is the right person to help you address your blockages. Highly reactive relationships are more destructive than anything, and should likely be brought to an end.

✳

If you're actively searching for a new relationship, the number one quality to look for in a potential partner is their ability to let you be you. When you get to be you, everything is easier. Committing is easier. Communicating is easier. Sharing, caring, and giving are easier. So is making love. Being there for each other in hard times is also easier. It's easier because you don't make your partner responsible for you feeling loved. Instead, your partner is the allowing presence for you to love yourself. You love them for giving you the space to be you, but self-love always comes first. It's from your own source of love that you can then love each other.

Usually, you can tell in the first few minutes of normal conversation where the balance lies. Are you comfortable in each other's presence? Do your interactions feel natural? Do you feel the need to defend your views? Or appease the other person? You don't need to be on the same page about everything. You just need to give each other the space to be yourselves. When that is the case, everything else falls into place.

The most challenging part of getting to know someone new is that it's easy for your mind to rule proceedings. It starts with your dating profile, where you list all your likes and dislikes. Things you agree with and disagree with. All your must-haves, nice-to-haves, and deal-breakers. You list everything from foods to moods, from virtues to vices. You think you're painting a picture of who you are and who your ideal mate is. But what you're actually doing, is listing all the ways you judge yourself and others.

Next, you search and compare profiles in hopes of finding someone whose judgments are similar to yours. Similar judgments make them more attractive, more trustworthy, more familiar. Consciously, greater judgment compatibility translates into less need for control. And subconsciously, it means a higher probability of getting what you want to compensate for what you lack.

Judgments about the future carry extra weight because they directly impact the outcomes your happiness depends on. Someone who has different projections is quickly cast aside. You would never want to depend on a person who doesn't share your opinions about a situation that hasn't happened yet. You would never want to wager your imagined future self's happiness on them. You need them to project the same beliefs into *their* unknown future because having the same future projections means you're on the same page now. Your filtered realities align.

If they don't, you can go separate ways, without feeling all too bad. It's an easy one to explain to family and friends. Your judgments are incompatible.

*

Everything comes back to being you. Your life flourishes when you're being you, and it falters when you're not. Relationships are no different. The freedom to be you is all you're striving for, whether you know it or not. When everyone gets to be themselves, opposites can get along splendidly. There's no need to argue because everyone is right. Your opinions don't have to line up because they're not important enough to defend. You don't argue about your plan for the future because you're not living for outcomes. Instead, you're letting love grow, one authentic moment at a time. You know that, however the road unfolds for you, it's the road you're meant to be on.

✳

Getting to a place of healthy independence is a significant milestone in your journey of self-realization. Whenever disagreements arise in your relationship, you're able to explore how stuck feelings, on either side, contribute to the situation. You no longer rely on each other to make you happy because everyone is their own source of happiness. Everyone is their own source of love. Of course, mutual care and affection are all part of good housekeeping. But you no longer put conditions on how or when love shows up. The fewer stuck feelings you have, the more you're able to receive love in whatever form it shows up because you already feel loved, in spades, by being you.

Once stuck feelings no longer dictate your relationship dynamic, what remains are the true points of compatibility:

lifestyle, physical chemistry, and mutual support. And if no one shows up that complements you in those ways, it's alright, too. Your pining to find that special person is over because you realize you've found that person in you.

✳

There may come a point in your journey of self-realization where you feel like you love everybody. While not romantic in nature, this love for all beings emerges when your self-love eclipses your previous sense of separateness. *When you no longer put conditions on the world to love you, you feel unconditional love for the world.*

Your relationship with yourself is the most important one of all. You are born alone, and you die alone. People you meet along the way are co-stars in your adventure of self-discovery. Love them with the fullest of hearts, for their journey is a part of yours. Thus, loving yourself is loving all.

FORGIVENESS

At first, forgiveness sounds like you're letting someone off the hook for what they've done. From that perspective, it's no wonder forgiveness is such a hard pill to swallow. Why should you ever forgive anyone for hurting you?

But forgiveness is never about others. It's always about releasing the negativity that's stuck inside of you from feeling hurt. Forgiveness is about healing yourself.

Of course, your mind thinks you're punishing the perpetrators for what they've done by continuing to hold them accountable. But all you're doing is punishing yourself by continuing to harbor negative feelings. You're hanging on to the pain, long after the actual event.

As long as you keep blaming, you keep hurting.

Forgiveness doesn't mean denying what has happened. Your hurt feelings are real. The point is not to perpetuate your pain. Whatever incident has happened is in the past.

Your choices are: release and move forward or blame and stay stuck. The longer you remain stuck, the more it consumes you, the more easily you get triggered. It's a vicious cycle.

No matter how obvious it may be that someone else is at fault, making them wrong never makes you feel better. It only makes you feel worse. Your insistence on being upset winds up superseding your health and happiness. You continue to feel like a victim long after the actual offense.

It's usually not until you've exhausted yourself by holding on to the hurt that forgiveness strikes you as an option. You're in such pain, you've reached the point where you no longer care about who's right and who's wrong. You just want it to be over. You've realized:

Forgiving is the only way for it to be over.

*

While forgiving others can be difficult, forgiving yourself can be even more challenging. Often, you have the highest expectations of yourself. Most of the pressure you feel in life is your own. You're the first to blame yourself and the last to forgive yourself. The inability to forgive yourself devolves into resistance to receiving love and kindness from others, no matter how overtly it is offered to you. Not only is self-forgiveness essential for releasing the pain, but it's also vitally needed so that self-love can flow again.

*

While the primary purpose of forgiveness is always to heal yourself, it can also heal those you forgive. Remember, they believe *their* side of the story. As long as they feel judged by you, they keep up a defensive shield that prevents them from reflecting on their own behavior. But when you let go of your insistence that you're right and they're wrong, they no longer have *you* to focus *their* blame on.

It's much harder to maintain animosity when nobody is pushing back.

Your non-resistance creates a mirror effect for others to reflect on their actions and their beliefs. All too often, people who hurt other people are acting out of their own pain. The negativity they generate towards you is a window into their inner world. When you cease to cast blame, you no longer present the outlet for their internal distress. They might find someone else to focus on, but there's also a chance they gain insight about themselves and come out of their suffering.

Whether or not that happens, however, is not your concern. Your focus should be on how *you* feel, not what anyone else is doing. If you expect others to atone, it's too easy to slip back into judgment. You start thinking you're doing all the heavy lifting, while they are oblivious to their actions, with no sign of remorse or desire to reconcile. Before you know it, you're back to blaming and bringing up old pain from the past. But as long as one party comes out of reactivity, there's a chance of healing for both sides.

*

The power of forgiveness can be incredible, sometimes even superhuman. Even in the most extreme cases of wrong-doing, people have managed to find forgiveness and release themselves from their victimhood. But as long as you continue to judge each other, everyone stays stuck. Everybody loses. Between people who judge each other, there can never be peace.

*

Ultimately, true forgiveness cannot come from the mind. It doesn't know how to forgive. It only knows how to create conditions. *I forgive you if...* Conditional forgiveness is only valid for as long as circumstances stay the same. If they change, the deal is off. And in a world that is always changing, that spells trouble. What's worse, if you look closely, deep down you're still hanging on to the pain.

Forgiving others isn't a conscious act. It's a natural byproduct of releasing the negativity you're holding on to.

*

Acts of forgiveness are acts of self-healing. They are an essential part of your journey of self-realization. There's no need to blame anyone, ever. Those who challenge you to forgive them push you to greater self-awareness. That's why don't forgive them for them. Forgive them for you.

LISTENING

If you've ever had a conversation with someone who's a good listener, you know how great it feels to receive undivided attention. It's healing to experience yourself thinking, talking, feeling, and expressing your emotions. You feel seen and heard, even more by yourself than the other person.

A good listener understands it's not about them. They sense if they bring *their* reactions into the mix, it interrupts your experience of yourself. It muddles the space in which you seek to process your feelings. A good listener's job is to be an unbiased mirror, so you can feel safe to be you.

*

To be a good listener, listen from your body awareness, not your headspace. Staying connected to sensations is key to staying present, attentive, and keeps you out of reactivity.

When you're present, you listen through your inner voice. Your inner voice is the ultimate supportive mirror because it holds everything as true. And there's nothing more important for the person sharing their feelings than to know their feelings are valid.

When you listen from your headspace, however, your truth structure keeps interfering with what you're hearing. Your head voices keep injecting themselves into the pure experience of listening. You run everything you hear through the filter of your own viewpoints in an ongoing effort to validate your beliefs. This diminishes the safe presence you're able to provide to the speaker. Even if you don't say anything, they can sense it. The quality of your attention drops. The speaker can see in your body language that you want to interject. Suddenly, they no longer feel heard. They feel judged. Instead of a healing experience, it can quickly escalate into a clash of opinions.

Always listen through your inner voice. It holds everything as true.

✳

Being a good listener doesn't just benefit the person sharing their feelings. The listener also experiences a deepening, simply from being a mirror. Bits and pieces of the listener's stuck feelings are also released as a result of witnessing the other person release theirs.

This is when you realize there is no separation. You can never assume another person's feelings to be separate from yours. Whenever you interact with anybody, you're engaging in an energy exchange. The less judgment there is on either side, the more energy is free to flow, and the more you help each other discover your authentic selves. Everyone benefits from good listening. But when you inject yourself into the other's experience, no one does.

✳

Being a great listener is one of the most powerful healing contributions you can make to the world. But even more important is to be a great listener to yourself. Ignoring your inner voice is the root of all your struggles. It's the only reason you ever feel lost, your life ever gets off track. Your inner voice responds to your circumstances. And your circumstances are always a reflection of you. Thus, when things are not going your way, it's you not going the way of things. When you're not getting the things you want, it's you not wanting the things you're getting. When you feel like life is not listening, it's you not listening to yourself.

Your inner voice is here to help you turn it around. The moment you stop judging yourself, the world stops judging you. The moment you love yourself, you feel loved by all. Your eternal happiness is already in place. All you have to do is listen.

LONELINESS

It shouldn't be so hard to be alone. After all, you've known yourself all your life. There hasn't been a single moment where you haven't been you. Surely, by now, the person you're most comfortable with is you.

But you've been ingrained with the belief that being alone is not okay. As a child, you're encouraged to go play with other kids because playing alone is seen as unhealthy. In school, the emphasis is on teamwork and collaboration. Socially, you're constantly being pressured to join some club and be part of some group. And while it's essential to learn to get along with others, it is equally, if not more important, to learn to get along with yourself.

You bring your relationship with yourself to everything you do.

✳

But society provides little opportunity for you to get to know yourself. Happiness is always depicted as people doing things together, whereas the connotations of being alone are mostly negative. If you live by yourself, you must be unhappy. If you enjoy solo activities, you must be hard to get along with. If you like eating out by yourself, you must not have friends. If you prefer to work alone, you must not be a team player. If you're not in a relationship, you must fear commitment. If you don't have kids, you must be selfish. And if your idea of fun is to read books about self-realization, you're just plain weird.

You can see why being with yourself can be so difficult to grapple with. The negative associations with being alone permeate all of society. When you misbehave as a child, you're sent to your room. As an adult, you're sent to solitary confinement. Being alone is considered the worst kind of punishment. Hence, the notion of spending time with yourself is easily misconstrued as *loneliness*, which can quickly devolve into *fear of loneliness*.

✳

See if you can observe your own fear of loneliness in everyday situations. Whenever there's a moment of solitude, you might feel the urge to check messages, put on some music, or call a friend for a chat. Socializing becomes the ultimate strategy for avoiding loneliness. From constantly going out, to keeping friends that hold you back, to not changing jobs because your coworkers are your social life, to not ending an unfulfilling relationship because being with *somebody* beats being alone. It's much easier to fill your calendar with things to do, places to be, and people to see than to spend time by yourself.

Even forced social interactions are better than none at all. Attend another wedding of someone you hardly know? *Sure!* Another birthday party of a friend of a friend? *Check.* Go see a bad movie? *Yes, please.* Even a bad movie is still better than staying home alone. At least you're enjoying the badness with a crowd. Anything beats being by yourself.

*

The stigma of *alone time* is so strong, it's not just about what others think. You can be your own worst critic. You're the first to think there must be something wrong with you when you're home alone or eating out by yourself; that you must be unlikeable if you don't have a big group of friends; that you must be unlovable if you're not in a relationship. You never begin to explore *me time* because you're so busy avoiding it.

Yet, *me time* is the most precious time of all. It's your time to step back from your busy life and focus on taking care of yourself. Your time to relax, replenish, and lose yourself in your favorite activities. Your time to feed your imagination through creative pursuits and expand your horizon of what's possible. Your time to watch the sunset and remind yourself of the beauty and simplicity of life. Your time to look up at the stars at night, in awe of the vastness of the cosmos and how crazy it is that you exist on this planet hurtling through space. Your time to reflect on the day and integrate the lessons you've learned, so tomorrow, you wake up a more complete you. All the insights the world reveals to you are lost if you don't take the time to reflect and be with yourself, intimately and honestly.

If there's ever a moment that calls for pure honesty, it's when you're facing yourself. There is nowhere to hide and nowhere to run. There is no one there to distract you from the feelings you've been avoiding. No one to comfort you in your discomfort. No one to wipe away your tears. No one to catch you if you fall into despair. You only have you. This is when you learn to be an ally, a confidant, a best friend to yourself. This is when you learn to love being you.

Learning to be alone is learning to be you.

✳

When you first sit down with yourself, you might not like what comes up. You might reject yourself, resent yourself, or even hate yourself. All the layers of self-judgment from years of avoiding your loneliness come into plain view. All the unpleasant parts, the fragmented pieces of a false self-image imposed on you by others who don't know you, rise to the surface. One of your life's biggest challenges is to come face-to-face with all the parts of yourself that you deem ugly. But once you do, something magical happens.

You realize nothing about you is ugly. Only your thoughts that say so are.

On the other side of your loneliness, your beautiful, unblemished, lovable self awaits. To get there, all you have to do is learn to get comfortable being by yourself.

Of course, there is great value in engaging with others, as well. It can be incredibly supportive and healing to talk with a best friend, confide in a family member, or work with a therapist. But the presence of others is only healing if it serves your self-reflection and doesn't distract you from being you.

*

The next time you're alone, notice the urge to look for the next distraction. Ultimately, loneliness is like any other feeling. Instead of fearing it, you can notice it, observe it, and release it. Let loneliness be the trigger that points to stuck feelings. By observing your sensations, you transmute self-rejection into self-acceptance, self-neglect into self-compassion, and self-loathing into self-love.

Life can only flow through you when you're at peace with being you. You know you're being you when you're comfortable being alone. Only then, in the absence of self-judgment, when the layers of your false self fall away, do you realize there is no separation between you and the moon and the stars. And when you're one with everything, you're never alone.

DEPRESSION

There is nothing more depressing than not being you. When you live in your head, listening to outside voices, comparing yourself to society's ideals, chasing your future happiness instead of being happy right now, it's no surprise that eventually you get depressed.

Depression happens when your life is not aligned with your truth.

Every single time you ignore your inner voice, it depresses your system. By the time physical symptoms of depression appear, it's the accumulation of countless instances of not being you.

As such, depression is a vitally important wake-up call to re-evaluate the place from which you live your life. It's a chance to reconnect with your inner truth and reboot as a more aligned version of you. Depression should never be treated as a problem that you need to get rid of. But rather, recognize its purpose of compressing you like a spring, so you can come out of it and expand with greater clarity and intention than ever before.

The longer you deny your truth, the deeper the depression, the bigger the reboot.

Rebooting can be stressful, of course. It involves letting go of all the beliefs that no longer serve you, as well as people, places, and things that are no longer aligned with who you are. But these growing pains are to be expected. If it were easy, you would reboot on your own, freely and willingly. Life would never have to force it upon you. In fact, it would never reach the point of a reboot in the first place, if you lived more continuously by your blueprint.

But never blame yourself for feeling depressed. And always remember, you don't have to deal with it alone. Establishing a support network or seeking professional help is an instrumental part of your journey of self-realization. It's all part of your expansion.

✳

Except for extreme cases of depression, resist the quick fix of managing your feelings with anti-depressants. Always first explore whether your symptoms can be alleviated using less intrusive means, such as breathing techniques, exercise, diet, rest, and various forms of therapy. Your body's intelligence has called for a reboot, and those are the things it needs the most. Medication may relieve symptoms, but it doesn't address the root cause of your depression: misalignment with your authentic self.

Once you're confronted with depression, the goal should never be to get back to your pre-depression state. Then nothing has changed, and the wake-up call has gone unheeded. You wind up dependent on chemicals to keep functioning, and the opportunity to shift into a more authentic place is lost.

Remember, all feelings have a purpose. They surface for a reason. Depression gives you the necessary push to make positive changes towards a better version of you. The you that doesn't seek distractions because you're comfortable being alone. The you that doesn't make the world responsible for how you feel. The you that doesn't need a perfect plan because you're excited to watch your path reveal itself. The you that isn't misled by what others say because your inner voice is loud and clear. The you that lives in awe and wonder because that's your natural state. The you that doesn't need to criticize because you see that everything is perfect just the way it is.

*

Ultimately, depression is like any other feeling. Giving it space to be is the quickest way to move through it, or rather, for it to move through you. It's suppressing and pushing away feelings that keeps them stuck. And stuck feelings are the root of all friction with life.

During times of reboot, be extra kind and gentle to yourself. Give yourself ample time to recalibrate. You're shedding old skin. Permanent repairs and upgrades are happening. Stay present with your sensations, and allow the depressed energy to work its way through your body and out of your system. You can trust your body's intelligence to work things out. Everything is happening for your highest good.

DRUGS

The universe has no intention of misleading you, confusing you, or making you feel lost. It doesn't benefit from annoying you, provoking you, or proving you wrong. There is no plot to withhold from you happiness, harmony, or life's innermost secrets. Rather, life has one simple job: to mirror how much or how little you're being you.

That's why when you're in conflict with yourself, life feels like a battle. When you're critical of yourself, you feel criticized by others. When you deny yourself happiness, the world makes you feel sad. Everything you experience in life is a reflection of you.

As such, doing drugs to cope with the world is entirely self-defeating. You're escaping reality as *you* see it through *your* filters. By numbing out you're not gaining the upper hand in life. You're not figuring anything out. You're running away from yourself.

✳

Life is designed to be a facilitator of self-awareness, healing, and growth. The next lesson to help you evolve is always at your doorstep. It comes to you, not because life somehow magically knows what you need to work on next, but because you continuously manifest your reality from your stuck feelings. The more stuck you are, the more you manifest lack, confusion, resistance. The less stuck you are, the more you manifest peace, harmony, acceptance. Who you are right now is always forcing the next step in your evolution. Look at your life currently, and see if you can tell where stuckness is playing its part.

✳

Depressants, like alcohol, lower your level of arousal. As a result, you experience relief from the pressure of living in your head and the restrictions social masks impose on you. You feel emboldened to cast aside self-judgments that limit your freedom of expression. Things that would normally trigger you, you're able to dismiss with a look of *whatever*.

But when you numb your senses, when you can no longer accurately feel your sensations, then you no longer notice feeling triggered. And that means you're no longer in sync with the primary feedback mechanism of life. What you perceive as relaxation and carefreeness is actually avoidance behavior, both from the mind's incessant need for control and from the messages coming from your inner voice that your life is out of whack.

Impaired senses make it impossible to feel and release stuck feelings. But that's the appeal of intoxication. The fact that your sensations are muted, your self-image distorted, and the mirror of life hazy, means you don't have to confront your filtered reality. You don't need to come to terms with a world that is showing you all the parts you dislike about yourself. Even if you know the escape is temporary, you'd rather not think about all the work required to heal. Because when you live in your headspace, all you want is relief from your headspace.

✳

On the other end of the spectrum are stimulants, like psychedelics, which boost your mood and exaggerate your senses. They, too, promise to help you shed your self-limiting beliefs so you can experience life without filters.

But no matter how elevating your high may be, no matter how compelling the revelations you encounter, no matter how much love and connectedness you experience, once you come back down, you have no practical foundation for holding your insights in an integrated way.

As everyday life returns, so do your old tendencies. You're back to clinging to feelings you like and resisting ones you don't. You're back to making plans and living for outcomes. You still believe you're right, and others are wrong. You still believe the world is to blame for your misery. Your happiest moments are planning the next escape to get back to your high, just so you can experience another glimpse of what it feels like to not judge yourself or others. In the meantime, the reality in front of you, the life you have manifested, that is designed to reveal your true self, is lost on you. Or rather, you are lost to life.

Stimulants might provide you with an experience of your uninhibited self, but bypassing the process of getting there, you miss the journey. And the journey is everything. It's your joy, your healing, and your self-realization. The journey is all there is and all that matters.

You can climb up the mountain or take a helicopter to the top. If you take the helicopter, you may come back with the same pretty photos. But you haven't developed stamina from the trek, gratitude for the adventure, or appreciation for the mistakes you've made. You neither have a grasp of the actual effort to help inspire others, nor the depth to show compassion for those who try and fail. Your character doesn't reflect the wisdom and integrity of overcoming hurdles. It can only reflect the fragmented self-image and brittle confidence of someone who has taken a shortcut.

By not climbing the mountain of your life, you miss out on your path. You can talk about the view from the top, but you've barely taken a step in your journey.

*

Escaping your reality doesn't help you discover yourself. Everyday situations do. Ecstatic insights don't reveal stuck feelings. The things that trigger you do. With every choice to be you, you contribute alignment, peace, balance, and flow to the world in a stable and contained way. But when you get high, the energy you engage with is erratic, fleeting, excessive, and chaotic. Not to mention, you are chemically reinforcing the belief that you are not enough.

You cannot get to the next layer of you without becoming conscious of the current layer first. Consciousness leads to acceptance, and acceptance leads to love.

Realize, there are no shortcuts you need to take. It's not about getting anywhere. It's all about realizing who you are right now, every step of the way.

✳

Ultimately, it's not about whether drugs are morally right or wrong. It's not about synthetic vs. organic. It's not about professionally administered micro-dosages. It's not even about your health. All of those things are just opinions in the context of social debate. What's missing is the realization that you live in a healing world, a loving world, an abundant world. A world that wants you to grow and prosper. That wants you to get unstuck and be part of the flow. A world that wants nothing more than for you to realize your inherent perfection.

Life is not out to get you, oppose you, or make things difficult. It never makes things harder than they need to be.

Everything is designed to push you towards greater alignment with your true self.

Drugs upset the world's desire for your alignment. They break your intimate, atomic-level connection to the reality around you, the reality that *is* you. They impair your ability to practice thought awareness and to release stuck feelings. They distort - and potentially destroy - your healing relationship with life. By getting high, you sabotage the self-realization process life has put into place.

Drugs interfere with life's process of revealing your perfection.

✳

Some might argue that drugs can be part of your journey. Of course, all experiences are valid. Your path can take any shape or form. Even if certain decisions take you off your path, the lessons learned eventually push you back onto it. It's just a question of *how many detours does your life need to take?* You have a say in that.

Your inner voice is here to guide you. As long as you listen, you can't go wrong. Even if you don't listen, you can't go wrong. Do what you must do. Just know, there is no greater high than being you.

MEMORIES

Just like expectations are attachments to the future, so are memories attachments to the past. Together, expectations and memories are the filters through which your mind interprets the present.

While expectations compare what is happening to what you think should be happening, memories work by judging what's in front of you based on experiences from the past. In other words, whenever a situation triggers a positive memory, you're inclined to see the present as positive. If there's a negative association, you're inclined to see it negatively. Even just meeting someone who has the same name as a person you like or dislike causes you to cast them in that particular light.

In short, both expectations and memories are core components of your mind's truth structure. They interfere with your experience of watching life unfold.

*

As memories accumulate, they become a measuring stick for how you feel about your life. The more positive memories you have, the better you feel about who you are. Keeping photos and souvenirs around reminds you of all the good times in the past, and a packed calendar full of fun events ensures you experience more of them in the future. Memories keep your controlling mind satisfied that life is good.

Memories are even more powerful when you get to share them with friends, family, the world. Now everyone gets to feel great about your life. Everyone gets to experience who you think you are. Some things you might never even do if it weren't for the chance to broadcast another fabulous selfie.

To the mind, creating memories is addictive because it represents knowing and control. Hence, it's common to want to create another great memory while the actual event is still happening. Go to any live event and you can see droves of people watching through the screens of their recording devices. You've probably done this yourself. And you might have noticed that the moment you switch from experiencing the event to capturing it, you're no longer part of it. You're already more connected to the memory of the moment than to the moment itself. You're experiencing the present as the projected past, even though you're still present, but not really. *That's a mind-bender.*

That doesn't mean you should forever abstain from capturing special moments. Just be aware that every time you look through a viewfinder, you're not really there. Find the appropriate time to capture the essence of a moment, but make sure experiencing it comes first. Otherwise, your great fear of missing out on life - the reason you create all those memories in the first place - comes true.

*

No matter how significant your memories may feel, no matter how much meaning they give your existence, if you take a closer look, you realize how remarkably inaccurate they are. This is where your mind's fickle nature is on full display. You can never recollect the same event in the same way twice. Your interpretation of *then* is always subject to the context of *now*. Everything from the mood you're in, to who you're talking to, impacts how you recount the past. Sometimes, you consciously alter details to better suit the situation. But more often, it's simply your fickle mind introducing some new variation, detail, or possibility. With so much volatility in your thoughts, it's only natural that memories continue to morph over time.

*

Just how much variation there is becomes apparent when you revisit memories you have in common with others. You quickly realize that people remember things differently, even when you grow up together in the same house. Even more remarkable is that everyone insists their version is the accurate one. Often, arguments over who's memories are right can be the hardest to resolve. No one wants to believe that the way they remember an event so integral to their personal history could be wrong.

It seems so silly from the outside, but when you're in it, letting go of *your* version of the past can be the most difficult thing because it threatens your identity. The threat of a modified past affecting who you think you are now looms large. So concerned are you with upholding your truth structure, you forget that it's never the actual event you remember. It's your interpretation of the event. A person standing right next to you, witnessing the exact same situation, is likely to have a completely different recollection of it. It doesn't matter if they are your sibling or best friend. No two people experience the same situation in the same way because everyone has different filters. Everyone has their own fickle mind.

If one person's memory is so volatile, you can imagine what happens over generations, centuries, millennia. Any event can be cast and re-cast in any light. Any figure can be made into a hero or a villain based on your current beliefs.

History is an entirely subjective retelling of the past from the perspective and predisposition of whoever is doing the retelling.

That doesn't mean you should reject the memories that you have. They are a part of who you are right now, and nothing about you should ever be rejected. But the more you work on releasing stuck feelings, the more any associated memories fade into the background. You find yourself less and less lost in thought, and less and less pining for things you are familiar with. Being you is the pure experience of being in touch with your sensations, responding to circumstances, unencumbered by thoughts of the past or future.

Memories play no role in you being you now.

Of course, it can be wonderful to reminisce about bygone days when the situation calls for it. Not every dinner with friends has to be about pure presence and existential philosophy. Just be aware that, if you derive meaning and identity from your memories, they become an artifact of clinging and resisting. They keep you stuck and out of sync with the flow.

✳

Every moment spent in your memories is a moment spent not being here. In contrast, every *new* experience passing through you leaves behind a deeper impression than the memory of the event ever can.

Just because you experience great moments doesn't mean you have to hold on to them. *Every* new moment is great, by virtue of its newness. The joy of life is letting it come and go. As one moment passes, the next one already awaits, and you get to be you all over again. Nothing can top that. Every moment of being you is as good as it gets.

WILLPOWER

Willpower is the hardest way to do anything, with the least chance for success. You think you're digging in your heels to ensure a particular outcome. But all you're doing is generating enormous resistance to circumstances that are pointing you elsewhere. Instead of tapping into the flow, you're setting yourself up for a long hard road. Nothing could be more antithetical to the joy and ease of being you.

*

Of course, society begs to differ. Willpower is generally thought of as a positive trait. It's a sign of strength and resilience. It means you're not easily deterred and that you don't throw in the towel when the going gets tough. The archetypical success story has the heroine seizing control of her destiny, doing whatever it takes to overcome her adversaries and impose her will on the world.

In everyday life, however, the hero mythos fades rather quickly. Navigating your circumstances on sheer willpower saps your energy, narrows your outlook, and eventually leads to burnout. All your actions feel heavy and desperate. There's no natural flow, no natural momentum pushing you along. Nothing gets done unless you will yourself to it.

In fact, the more willpower you apply, the more your momentum ceases. Just like the more you resist something, the more it bogs you down. But despite all signs to the contrary, the mind wants what it wants, because what it wants is control. It makes you believe you're taking charge of your destiny. But all you're doing is living for outcomes while taking the path of *most* resistance.

✳

Using willpower is so difficult, an entire industry exists dedicated to the subject of habit-forming. Indeed, when something becomes habitual, your mind is less likely to interfere, and because you're doing things more or less automatically, you execute tasks with less resistance. The correlation is accurate:

The less you think, the more likely you are to flow.

But as anyone who has tried to form a new habit can attest to, it's easier said than done. That's because habit-forming takes the outside-in approach. In other words, by changing your behavior on the outside, you seek to change how you feel on the inside. No doubt, repetition, structure, and discipline can have a very positive impact on your productivity and well-being. But transforming yourself from the outside-in is not the natural way of the world. Life is designed to be your mirror. Manipulating the mirror to shift your internal frequency is a tremendously difficult undertaking. That's why it takes forever to form good habits. It's possible, of course. But why struggle with habits and willpower when your inner voice is the path of *least* resistance?

You don't have to push. You don't have to steer. All you have to do is listen.

Listening to your inner voice and taking clear action is so easy, so smooth, it feels like you're executing a script. That's because you are - the script of *you*. Every experience reveals more of who you already are. To be you is never to force your way to anything. It's to let your life unfold perfectly on its own.

SURRENDER

Surrender is the act of giving up control. Not that you have control over anything in life, ever. But when you're in your headspace, you believe that you do. You keep controlling, planning, steering, and living for outcomes. And then you get frustrated when things don't go your way. Eventually, after trying to bend the world to your will has gotten you nowhere, you hit a wall. You might even hit rock bottom. That's when surrender becomes an option.

Initially, surrendering brings peace to your exhausted mind. But it's a misleading sense of calm. Underneath the surface, your mind never actually lets go. That's because everything the mind creates is part of its controlling nature, including a temporary letting go. Even if you're entirely convinced that you've given up control over a situation, it's usually just conditional. The moment conditions change, so does your willingness to surrender.

But don't blame yourself. That's just the way your mind works. Surrender is a foreign concept. It cannot accept it forever. Indeed, quietly, a different kind of anguish is building up. Deep down, the belief that your way is the best way is still there. As soon as the opportunity presents itself, the desire to control comes bubbling up, and your never-really-gone steering mindset comes roaring back.

Your mind does not know how to surrender. You can only come out of your head altogether.

✳

Similar to surrender, *tolerance* is another attempt by your mind to buy itself a timeout from the burden of continuous judging. The very definition of tolerance, however, implies your sense of superiority is alive and well. You're tolerant of others, but you clearly still think you're right. You're just giving others permission to be wrong. At least there is something pacifist about surrender. You are backing down from the fight. But a person who tolerates is always ready to throw punches.

Even *patience* is a tactic by your mind to relieve itself of the pressure of always having to be right. It's a temporary truce with itself that permits others to be wrong for the time being. But in that span of patience, your mind is looking for a more subtle way to convey what it thinks is the truth. Because secretly, it wishes nothing more than to tell the whole world how to behave. The fact that the world doesn't listen to you, is one of your biggest stressors.

*

Of course, some personal growth can still happen even with conditional surrender. That's because you go through a lot to get to the point of relinquishing control. While the break from steering is only temporary, it does present a window of opportunity for insight and self-reflection.

Be mindful, however, that your sneaky mind doesn't start controlling again sooner than you think. Often, there's an underlying expectation that accompanies surrender. You think you're ok with letting whatever wants to happen, happen. But if you look closely, you're still hoping whatever you wanted to have happen, happens. The mind still wants what it wants, even when you think you've given up.

As long as you live in your headspace, you cannot escape the control of your mind.

*

When you're connected to your sensations, however, listening to your inner voice, there is no such thing as surrender. There is only flow. There is only exploring what resonates in the here and now. How you feel in this moment is your best predictor of how you feel in the next one. Go with the flow, and you can be sure that your most extraordinary life isn't just on its way, it's already here.

FAILURE

Failure is when the outcome you've been living for, based on a goal that isn't yours, doesn't match the expectations stemming from making decisions not in alignment with you. If that sounds like a mouthful of nothingness, that's because it is. There is no such thing as failure. It only feels like there is when you're in your headspace, focused on outcomes. But when you're not focused on outcomes, there is only living, learning, doing, and letting go.

*

Growing up in a fear-based society, however, you're taught to avoid failure at all costs. First, you are confronted with parental expectations and the pressure to not let them down. Then the education system instills fear and self-loathing in you in the form of grades and report cards. Later in the workplace, you are judged with performance reviews. You carry this failure mindset into your senior years, judging yourself when your mental and physical faculties naturally start to slow down.

✳

Feeling like you've failed can be so final, so absolute, it's easy to forget that whatever constitutes failure is entirely subjective. To the person who is trying to please outside voices, failing is an absolute disaster. For the student working on letting things come and go, it's a great learning opportunity. And for the master who is in the flow, it's an enriching gift that eventually passes. There's nothing ever to be gained from vilifying the experiences that help you realize yourself more.

Judging yourself for failing is like punishing yourself for learning and growing.

You don't learn to walk by staying down when you fall and berating yourself for why you've fallen. The path of least resistance is to get up and try again. Through simple trial and error, you develop better skills, better insight, greater empathy, and compassion for others. That's how you discover what's true for you. It's cause and effect. Failing means you're doing. And you realize yourself through the doing.

✳

Reframing failure as something positive and necessary can be challenging, but learning to deal with the *fear of failure* can be even more daunting.

Fear of failure is one of the great inhibitors of being you. It impacts your entire life. When you fear failure, you see less opportunity to succeed and more chances to disappoint. Instead of relying on your strengths, you focus on your perceived shortcomings. Creativity ceases to flow and life feels more like a battle than an adventure. You cling to a version of reality you deem *safe* and surround yourself with others who reaffirm your fear-driven views.

But what really makes fear of failure so menacing is that it arises before you actually fail. Your mind projects how actions you haven't taken might impact a future you can't predict. The fear of negative consequences - of what *could* happen - is often more stressful than it actually happening.

When you focus on everything that could go wrong, you feel like you've already failed.

It's somewhat ironic that the mind strives to play it safe because playing it safe is what fuels your fear of failure. The more removed you are from taking action, the more you stay stuck in the mental theoretical realm, where the possibilities of projecting, predicting, and fearing all that might happen are endless. That doesn't mean you should act recklessly or take exceptional risks. Self-care is part of conscientious doing. But if you don't get off the couch, your inner voice can't come through to guide you.

✳

You find yourself in the doing. And because there's never anything wrong with being you, the more you do, the more you become immune to fear of failure. You grow in confidence to experiment, explore, and be curious. Finding out what works for you, not what others think of you, becomes your primary orientation. Instead of focusing on outcomes, you're focused on continuous learning.

Living for outcomes is not living. Outcomes happen while living.

✳

The next time you experience the agony of failure, notice where you feel it in your body. Stay focused on your sensations until they dissolve. Resist the urge to analyze the situation, you can always do that later. For now, the first order of business is to release your feelings and allow your reaction to pass. Only then can you see the situation for what it is and take clear action.

Perhaps you discover that you need to prepare better. Or maybe you realize your heart isn't in it, and this is your opportunity to shift into a more authentic place. Whatever it may be, nothing is gained from letting yourself plummet into shame and despair. Failure only exists in your mind.

When you listen to your inner voice, failure isn't even a thing. You can't fail when you're not attached to outcomes. You can't let anyone down when you're not trying to meet their expectations.

You can't lose when you're being you.

✳

Let life be easy, light, and fun. Because when you don't interfere with the flow, that's what it is. Every new moment is fresh, exciting, and invigorating. You're living and learning. You're letting solutions outweigh problems and opportunities outshine obstacles. You're making decisions that are passionate, free-flowing, and connected to life.

The more you're connected to life, the more you relish the natural order of things. You're aware that the world is your playground and that you create the circumstances through which you realize yourself more. You know you live in a perfect system.

Stay open to all of life's possibilities because when you no longer fear them, you realize you're one of them.

HOPE

The conventional take on *hope* is that it's an expression of optimism in the face of adversity. It's what heart-warming, feel-good stories are all about. You hope for a better future, hope that things turn out well. Who wouldn't want a happy ending? But look closely and you can see that hoping is a form of pushing away the present, as well as clinging to a more desirable outcome of the future. And whenever the keywords *clinging* and *outcome* are involved, you can be sure you're in your headspace.

Hope is fundamentally rooted in lack. To hope is to say the present isn't good enough and you would rather put all your faith into tomorrow. Instead of responding to your circumstances and taking clear action, you focus on future outcomes and stay in resistance to now.

Ultimately, hope is another coping mechanism of your mind to deal with feeling out of control.

Certainly, hope can energize and motivate you to keep moving forward. It can alleviate anxiety in times of crisis. But you would experience a lot less crisis by staying present, to begin with. The main reason you hope for better days is that your hyper-controlling mind is always in resistance to what's in front of you now.

At best, hope might alleviate the intrinsic stress and confusion of being disconnected from your inner voice. At worst, it reinforces feeling disempowered and keeps you in a state of reactivity, unable to take clear action.

Hope keeps you attached to wishful outcomes.

✳

The more you realize yourself, the less you hope. The world doesn't seem out of control because you're not trying to control the world. You flow effortlessly, even as your circumstances change. You no longer linger on things that have already happened because you've internalized that everything you experience has already happened. Hopes and dreams and wishes all fall away because being part of the happening is so much bigger, so much more compelling than all your hopes and dreams and wishes. Being in the moment is being part of all there is. What more could you hope for?

Immense relief and freedom follow when you no longer need to hope. Instead of wishing your life to be different, you're firmly grounded in being you right now.

Why hope for feeling better in the future, when being you now is the best feeling there is?

✳

Listen to your inner voice and let circumstances lead the way. Everything you need to learn and grow is contained in the reality you continuously manifest for yourself. There is nothing left to hope for because everything is perfect the way it is. And the way it is is perfect because it's you.

COINCIDENCE

Coincidence is a label your mind puts on events it cannot explain. It's part of the effort to keep making the unknown known. By calling something a *coincidence*, everything else that's not a coincidence appears to be under control.

There's a big bucket of similar words that are all part of your mind's toolbox to keep upholding its truth structure. Words like luck, chance, fluke, synchronicity, destiny, and fate all serve to explain away the unexplainable so that you can keep planning and steering towards the outcomes you think lead to happiness. Even describing something as an *accident* is more acceptable and soothing to the mind than allowing for the possibility of not knowing why.

This strategy only works, however, as long as there aren't too many coincidences. They must be the exception to the rule. If too many unpredicted things happen in a short span of time, it can quickly feel like chaos and start to overwhelm you. Your truth structure starts to crumble, revealing your greatest fear of all: that you don't have control over your life.

Which you don't. But this is only a problem when you live in your headspace because your mind operates on knowing and controlling. It goes to extreme lengths to create the illusion of control. Feeling out of control gives rise to your deepest existential fears. All the *bad* things that *could* happen come rushing in.

The obsession with trying to control your life originates entirely in the mind. The predicament is that you never come out of it long enough to realize there is another place from which you could live your life. You're so busy avoiding your fears, flow never gets a chance to take hold.

$$*$$

Everything your mind creates is in support of the illusion of control. Your entire filtered reality is an imaginary world. Your mind creates this projection - not because it wants to fool you - but because that's the best it can do. You're using a limited tool to make sense of unlimited life.

To be fair, your mind does a pretty amazing job. After all, it's trying to slay the dragon that is the unknowable cosmos. It creates the past, avoids the present, and projects the future. It takes the nothingness it fears and turns it into something it thinks it can control. Without a doubt, your mind is a clever tool. It goes to work, compensates for its shortcomings, and figures out a way to survive.

But you're here to do more than just survive.
You're here to thrive.

Your inner voice is your master guide. It doesn't need to explain away the unexplainable by calling it coincidence. It's not obsessed with making the unknown known. It only deals with what exists right now, which is the reality in front of you. Which is you.

You know you're on your path because an unmistakable trust emerges. Nothing in or around you feels accidental. That's because it isn't. You're living from one unfolding moment into the next, taking clear action along the way. Every step in your journey is backed by your fully realized self. You don't need to rely on luck or coincidence because nothing is more intentional than being you.

NATURE

Nature doesn't judge. Rocks, plants, animals, from the raging river to the busy microbe, all things get to be themselves. That includes you. Nature never tells you to be any different. It accepts you just the way you are.

Have you ever gone for a walk in the forest and felt criticized by the trees? If anything, it's the opposite. It feels like the trees welcome you. They *want* you to be you because you are an expression of nature just like they are. You are not separate from them. But when you're in your headspace, you think you are.

*

It's not surprising that growing up in a world built by and for the headspace, the connection to your natural roots gets cut. All the major institutions of modern life inflate the importance of the mind, committing you to a life lived for outcomes, separateness and identification with your truth structure. The relentless focus on knowledge creates the illusion that you are above nature, that you control it, instead of seeing yourself as an expression of it.

Furthermore, living in urban settings you become so distant to the natural world, that you think you're here and nature is over there. You only notice it when you *go into nature* while the rest of your time is spent largely removed from it.

Even when you do engage with nature, you think it exists to serve you. Whenever you want something from it, do you ask for permission? Or do you just take?

Only when you think of yourself as separate do you forget that plants have feelings, too. Animals are sentient beings, just like you. And even the rock has an energy about it. But as long as you live through the mind, as long as you label things as *other,* you're able to do to others what you would never do to yourself.

Deep down, however, you *are* doing it to yourself. You're hurting yourself by seeing yourself as separate from the life forms around you. Any act of culling other living beings, any mindless exploitation of natural resources, no matter how small or insignificant it may seem, is ultimately a violation of the life force that runs through you, too. The only time another life can seem insignificant is when you're in your headspace, cut off from your inner voice.

By disrespecting nature you disrespect yourself.

But despite any abuse, nature doesn't hold a grudge. It doesn't give you grief. The moment you show it some love, the moment you give it space to be, nature comes roaring back to life, providing you with all the nurturing elements that make you healthy and happy.

When you spend time in nature, you can feel its healing presence. Your connection to the flow returns. You can feel curiosity and creativity awaken. You see the impeccable order of things and how all elements work together to form a balanced, self-sustaining habitat. Every blade of grass contributes to the balance by being itself, for which it receives nourishment, structure, and purpose in return. You experience that same balance, well-being, and purpose in return for being you.

Cultivating self-love begins with cultivating love for all of life. Even the smallest insect contains the same desire to be what it's meant to be that exists within you. The same intention that has gone into you has gone into it.

You are made *with* a flourish and made *to* flourish. Find the beauty and perfection of nature in yourself. It's waiting for you to realize it's always there. Go and be with nature. Go and be with you.

TIME

Time enables you to experience everything that makes the physical world so compelling. Beginnings and endings. Departures and returns. Ascent and descent. Conception and completion. Inception and transformation. And last but not least, life and death. Time enables you to be in your body and leave your body. In more ways than one, you're here to experience time.

✳

On the one hand, time is very practical. It's helpful to know how much time it takes to boil an egg or get from point A to point B. Because of time, you know when to leave for work in the morning, when to plan vacations, and when to send out invitations for your birthday party. Time provides the logistical backdrop for all organizational matters.

On the other hand, there is the conceptual side of time, primarily consisting of the past and future. This is where your life gets complicated.

At first, the past and future seem like an undeniable part of your existence. Without a past, you wouldn't have an identity, and without a future, you wouldn't know where your identity is headed. You can't imagine life without knowing your past and future.

But that's precisely the point. Past and future are purely mental concepts. They are virtual canvases the mind creates upon which it projects its stories. Whenever you get lost in thought, it's your mind jumping around seamlessly between the canvases of time, interconnecting and weaving projections into an elaborate personal narrative. The core experience of being in your headspace is living *from* who you think you are and *for* who you think you should be.

✳

That's why a simple task like focusing on your breath is such a struggle. Your mind is used to operating in the endless imaginary realm of the past and future where it has full reign to project whatever it needs. But suddenly, you're asking it to focus on the breath coming in and out of your nose and be content with that? No wonder your mind freaks out. No wonder it rebels. There's nothing for it to do. There's no opportunity to steer, rationalize, or judge; no possibility of getting lost in the filtered reality of yesterday and tomorrow; no way to cover up all the feelings you've been avoiding; no way to create drama around what is happening because you want it to happen differently. No wonder your mind does everything it can to pull you back into your headspace, into the conceptual realm of time. That's where it rules you. That's where it has all the power.

When you attempt to take that power away, your mind goes into survival mode. It deploys an army of fears, doubts, and opinions. It wants you to keep defending your truth structure. It wants you to keep pushing away feelings. It wants you to keep pursuing predictability. And most of all, it wants you to keep believing in permanence.

Permanence is your mind's core belief. It's built into the simplest language you use. *I am a good person. You are a bad person. My teacher is great. Your dog is cute.* These are all statements that extend into infinity. They are single impressions declared as permanent truths. And in an ever-changing world, nothing shuts down your flow faster than saying something is something forever. Nothing creates more conflict than trying to impose permanence on an impermanent world.

When you demand permanence from a world where none exists, you suffer.

*

Oddly enough, your mind should know that permanence is nowhere to be found when it comes to the future. There isn't a plan you make that doesn't need to be continuously reinforced and vehemently defended against the relentless tide of change. You would think by now you realize that the future cannot be predicted, let alone planned for. But no matter how exhausting and futile, the effort to discover the holy grail of permanence continues. It's just because that's how your mind works.

That's also why your mind loves spending time in the past. The past is irrevocable, irrefutable, set in stone. Your mind gets to relax because nothing needs to be invented. Everything already exists. It's a popular notion that *you can't change the past, but you can change your future.*

But this is an entirely mind-based perspective. You think you know the past because it consists of events that have already happened. But it's not past events that you remember. It's your interpretation of those events. And all interpretations are subject to change.

When everything is essentially an opinion, it becomes clear there's no such thing as objective truth. Events and how you feel about them are two separate things. As such, even the past is never absolute. Every time you release stuck feelings, it impacts your interpretation of life. That means you can absolutely change the past. In fact, a big part of healing trauma consists of reframing your story about it.

The past is just a collection of stuck feelings.

That said, replacing one interpretation of an event with another can only get you so far. It helps, of course, to reframe your beliefs from something negative to something more positive. But, ultimately, beliefs are beliefs. As long as you're in your headspace, you're still subject to the controlling nature of your mind. You're still imprisoned by your truth structure. True healing and true freedom result from coming out of your headspace altogether and letting go of *all* interpretations of the past.

Only when you're free of the past are you free to experience yourself right now.

✳

Your fully realized self does not exist in the past, nor does it live in the future. You can only be you in your present circumstances because you *are* your circumstances. How you perceive the world is always how you perceive yourself. All possibilities exist until you create constraints by setting expectations. You are the master of your own limitations.

Your true nature is as limitless as the ever-expanding cosmos. To be in non-resistance to the flow, is to be in non-resistance to yourself. And when you no longer resist being you, time ceases to exist. Be you and be timeless.

PLAY

To be at play is to be doing without thinking, responding without resisting. Sublime tranquility comes over you, and you are completely present. You're flowing with the pace, shifting with ever-changing conditions. You're executing with utmost clarity and to the highest of your ability. Play is fun because it takes you out of your head and into your body. When you play, you get to be you.

The moment thoughts interfere, however, your whole experience falls apart. Suddenly, you're disconnected from your environment. You're no longer just doing. You fall out of sync with your body and miss essential cues. You start fumbling, tripping, getting nervous. You find yourself hoping that somebody else makes a mistake before you do. The joy of flowing gives way to the fear of what could happen, which then is more likely to happen because you're putting your attention there.

The game of life is no different. Your mind is always in fear of making mistakes, of not doing the right thing. There is an undercurrent of constant anxiety. But if you stay connected to your body and follow your inner voice, you experience all the benefits of being in the flow: harmony, clarity, continuity, excitement, and wonder. Where others see obstacles, you see opportunities. Where others dread the thought of tomorrow, you're excited to see what comes next. Where others argue over their piece of the pie, you relish being part of something much bigger than just yourself. To be you is to be on the same team as life, collaborating, facilitating, participating in the continuous unfolding of everything at the moment of its manifestation.

Life rewards everyone who plays by its rules. The rules are clear. Be you and prosper.

✳

Remember, life is designed so you cannot lose. You cannot fail. The cards are not stacked against you. There is no opposition, other than you getting in your own way. And should you stumble, life helps you get back on your feet, as long as you listen. As long as you stay present in your body, maximum flow is available at all times.

To be you is to be *in the zone*. It is to be at the peak of your powers. The less you resist the rules, the faster and more magnificently your true self unfolds. In the game of life, everyone who is true to themselves wins. Those who are not, have to wait a bit longer.

AGE

Age is so much more than just a number. It is the single-most self-limiting belief of your life.

Age-related programming accompanies you throughout your entire lifetime. Childhood, youth, adulthood, senior citizenship - these broad labels come bundled with highly specific, deeply ingrained beliefs and expectations, most of which you're not aware of until you get there. Wherever you are in your life, age-related norms exist for practically everything: health, wealth, looks, career, knowledge, social etiquette, relationships, and self-image.

The pressure from these age norms is relentless. You find yourself in constant comparison to what *others your age* are doing, how they look, where they are in life, whether they're better off or doing worse, whether you're ahead of them or falling behind. You keep looking for proof from people your age or older who are achieving things you still want to achieve, to fuel your hopes that there's still time to give your dreams a shot.

But the clock in your mind is always ticking. You can never get ahead of it, you can only try to keep up. The best you can do is meet society's expectations. Everything else is falling short. Keeping up with social expectations is the bane of your existence. It's your biggest source of stress and your biggest distraction from being you.

Nothing ages you faster than living by who you think you should be.

✳

Age norms don't just stress you out mentally and emotionally. The attitudes you pick up about aging have a direct impact on your physical well-being. Every time you hear someone explain away an ache or pain by saying *this is what happens when you get old*, it programs you to expect that to happen when you reach their age. Your anticipation of what life is like at certain stages has a significant say in it actually turning out that way.

The most important thing to remember is that statistics are averages of others. The uniqueness of every individual gets lost. Ultimately, you have your own life to live, with your own circumstances, your own stuck feelings, your own blueprint. No two people live the same life. The only thing everyone has in common is that they're on the journey of self-realization.

The more you choose to be you, the more you dislodge yourself from the external age grid, and the healthier, more free-flowing you become. When you're firmly grounded in *your* experience of life, you are free to let others have their own. You know that releasing stuck feelings and listening to your inner voice is the best thing you can do for your health and happiness now and every moment to come.

When you're in the fold of new moments coming and going, life happens right on time. There's no other time it can happen, anyway. And that applies to you, too. You can only be you now. There is nowhere else that's real. So be grateful for every sunrise and every sunset, not because it could be your last, but because you're experiencing it. It means you're real. It means you're eternal. It means you're being you. Be you and be ageless.

BLACK SHEEP

Sometimes the most challenging part of being you is that your own family doesn't accept you for who you are. They feel threatened by you because you want to take a different route than the commonly accepted one. They are quick to ridicule you for going against the family grain, even if that means accepting dysfunctional dynamics passed down through generations.

Whenever you break away from the ingrained behavior of a group, you expose their stuck feelings. They then blame you for causing them discomfort, but there's not much you can do. It's futile to try and educate others about stuck feelings if they're not prepared to look at themselves. The journey of self-realization cannot be forced. It unfolds for everyone at their own time, at their own pace, just like it has for you. You can't impose your path onto others. All that does is create resistance and conflict.

✳

But there's little consolation in knowing this when your relationship with your family reaches toxic levels. It can be one of the most upsetting life situations when the people who are supposed to love you and support you are the ones holding you down.

When dealing with toxic family members, your primary objective should be self-care. Establish healthy boundaries, so the toxicity doesn't pull you in. If that means distancing yourself completely, so be it. You shouldn't compromise your sanity for anyone, regardless of whether you're related. The desire to fix unhealthy family dynamics may come from a good place, but it can keep you entangled in reactivity indefinitely. Sometimes you just have to accept that if your family rejects you for who you are, you have to find your tribe elsewhere, at least for the time being.

That doesn't mean you should give up on your relatives, no less than you should give up on any human being. Just realize that they have their path, and you have yours. You cannot force them to align. See your situation for what it is, and take clear action from there.

✳

The good news is, if just one person comes out of their reactivity and stops feeding the cycle of blame, healing can happen for all. In fact, some positive change is virtually guaranteed. But it starts with each individual healing themselves. You must break the unhealthy patterns within yourself first, so you don't trigger them in others.

Your primary responsibility in life is always towards your own stuck feelings. That's the one thing you can impact for yourself, and that's the one thing that has the most impact on others.

You cannot change others, but you can change yourself. That changes others.

The essence of being you is something everyone is seeking. It's what everyone is after. When others see you at peace with yourself, you become an example for them to find peace within themselves. Don't expect others to change when you change yourself. But don't be surprised if they do.

＊

As always, forgiveness plays a vital role in your healing. Your inner voice doesn't resent you for not listening to it, so why should you harbor resentment when others don't listen to you? Holding grudges only hurts yourself.

No matter how stuck others appear to be, healing is always a possibility, and shifts c an occur at various stages of life. Always stay open to the possibility of change, in them, as much as in yourself.

Trust in their journey of self-realization, as much as you trust in yours.

✳

If you feel like an outsider in life, don't let it hold you back. Realize you are on a bigger mission. You're the one who can break the unhealthy patterns. You're the one called to heal the wounds that no one else can. You're the one determined to take your life in a new direction, to make a difference for yourself, and everyone else.

Let them call you the black sheep of the family. Wear it as a badge of honor. Accept the limits of your relationship with family and friends, but always be compassionate towards the pain of others.

Ultimately, everybody has a unique path. Ultimately, everybody is a black sheep. The only difference is, some don't know it yet. But you do. Be the black sheep. Be you.

DEATH

Death is the ultimate highlight of life. To get to experience the transition from the physical back into the non-physical is the grand finale. It's even more compelling than the experience of being born because you take a more realized version of yourself back with you.

Of course, the more stuck feelings you have, the less thrilling the idea of leaving your body is. Stuck feelings keep you attached to the physical dimension. They are the hopes and dreams you cling to, the outcomes you pursue, and the expectations you've hinged your happiness on. All the things you're still hoping to get done represent stuck feelings. Because if they didn't, you'd have no problem letting them go.

*

With so much unfinished business, it's no wonder that something as unpredictable, uncontrollable, and seemingly final as death doesn't sit well. Leaving your body behind means the end of wanting, predicting, expecting, and controlling. It means the end of your life as you know it. Or rather, as your mind knows it.

Death is the great unknown, and since your mind operates on knowing things, there couldn't be a greater threat than the idea of permanently not knowing. Hence, if there's ever a thought you push away, it's about death. Your mind refuses to deal with it until it comes knocking, and when it does, it's the most unwelcome guest ever.

Until that day arrives, your mind's top concern is to keep itself distracted from the unknown, by focusing on the known. That's why anticipating the next shoe sale or debating a sporting event is much more compelling than contemplating your own death. It's remarkable that you spend most of your life *not* thinking about dying, considering you're guaranteed to die, and that you don't know when. For all the elaborate plans you make, you never spend time considering your inevitable exit. Instead, you act like you're meant to live forever.

Because the moment you consider it, everything would shift. The things you spend time on. The people you spend time with. The way you treat your body. The lifestyle choices you make. How freely you share your blessings with others. How much you appreciate differences. How much you love your planet. How much you love yourself.

The moment you stop taking life for granted, suddenly, you're as authentic as can be.

✳

As long as you live in your head, you get caught up in the minute details of judging, reacting, and steering, blind to the miracle of it all. Your mind's resistance to death doesn't just make life difficult when the time comes, it makes your whole life difficult in the meantime. Stuck feelings about death are the most fundamental form of resistance to life. There is enormous stress in thinking of death as this abrupt, radical event that puts an unwanted end to your physical existence. Yet, you keep pushing it away, all the while living in constant fear of it.

You cannot enjoy living as long as you fear dying.

Society doesn't make your relationship with death any easier. On the contrary. Major industries exist that urge you to fight the aging process. The general attitude values youth over seniority, a long life over a short one. An accidental death is portrayed as tragic. Even when it happens naturally, it's always unfortunate.

When you're surrounded by so much aversion to death, it's no wonder you feel like it always happens too soon, you're never ready for it, and the best you can hope for is that it happens quick and pain-free.

✳

For many, dealing with their own death is easier than dealing with the potential or actual death of others. When someone close to you dies, it can be devastating, especially when it happens suddenly. Of course, it's natural to grieve the loss of a loved one. You miss the connection to their physical presence in your life. But the greater emotional difficulties stem from unresolved stuck feelings. All your attachments and avoidance behaviors become exposed, along with the fear that you're left to deal with all of it on your own. While healing is always possible, it's a lot more work to release stuck feelings with the other person no longer present. All the more reason to make the effort to reconcile while they still are.

＊

Your strongest position in life is to have a daily practice of releasing stuck feelings before they build up. That way, the next time a loss occurs, it can be a genuine celebration of life and not a sudden confrontation with painful emotions.

As for your own death, it's in your best interest to go into the final curtain call with as few stuck feelings as possible. Any unresolved energy that remains, lives on in the impact it has on the people around you, just like you have been impacted by the stuck feelings of others before you. Complete non-resistance is being called for. Your greatest gift to the ones you leave behind is your full acceptance of the end of your physical life. To be at peace at the time of your passing is to leave behind a legacy of compassion, love, honor, and dignity. By doing so, you empower others to take these qualities into their lives and into their final breath.

*

The more you embrace the flow of life, the more you experience yourself as continuous. Your fear of death subsides because you recognize yourself to be bigger than your physical existence. For however long your life may last, whatever shape it may take, you know every moment has utmost significance by virtue of being part of the great coming and going.

The fact that time in the physical is shorter for some, longer for others, does not diminish their life's significance or impact on the world. Every moment you choose to be you, you're fulfilling the impossibly grand desire behind life's blueprint. Every time you listen to your inner voice, it's a validation of the love for creation.

To be you is to fulfill your life's purpose and to fulfill the purpose of life.

*

Everything in life comes and goes. There are no exceptions. Your body is your vehicle. You drive it for a while until you return it to the dealer. There is undoubtedly a system in place. You call it *the circle of life* for a reason.

Fear of physical suffering during the dying process is understandable. Nobody wants to be in pain. But the greater existential fear stems from your mind's need for control. Hence, losing control seemingly forever is your greatest nightmare. But the moment you come out of your headspace and embrace not knowing, you are free to flow with life, beyond the constraints of your mortal existence.

It's not necessary to know what happens once you leave your body. Only your mind needs to know. Instead, honor each moment as it comes. When you take away your expectations of what it should be, you feel continuously alive, connected, loved. You feel like you're eternal because there's no end to the continuity.

Your journey of self-realization is about learning to let all things come and go. That includes your physical being. Your greatest contribution to life is to go into death being you. Be you and be intrigued about what comes next.

PART III

The Big Picture of Being You

SUFFERING

You always emerge from a period of suffering as a deeper, wiser, more grounded, more compassionate human being. You feel more wonder for the impossible miracle of your existence, more gratitude for every precious moment you have, more acceptance that every person in your life is a blessing - your friends, as well as your foes. But most of all, you come out of it more of you. Suffering is life's built-in cleansing process to encourage you to release stuck feelings and help you realize who you truly are.

*

You suffer because you think the world is keeping you from living the best life you can imagine, not realizing you can't imagine your best life.

When your plans aren't working out, life doesn't want you to give up. It wants you to dream bigger, dig deeper, fall harder, rise stronger, and trust yourself more. It's saying let go and let the flow take you to where you're meant to go, in ways you can never imagine going. Life wants you to be you *so much,* only when you're *not* being you, does it give you a kick in the butt. It's tough love, but it works.

✳

The more you let go of beliefs about what your life should be, the less you get kicked in the butt. You no longer have to wait for your life to get difficult. You no longer need to experience another truth crisis. You can cut down on the vast majority of your suffering without having to go through it. Most of it is not extreme, anyway, if you nip it in the bud. It's the ongoing stream of daily annoyances accumulating inside of you that eventually pushes you over the edge. But by taking the time to observe and release stuck feelings regularly, you prevent them from building up, and most of your suffering never happens.

That doesn't mean difficult situations don't continue to happen. Deadlines at work are stressful. A relationship breakup hurts. Losing a loved one causes heartache. And physical injuries are painful. But when you give difficult feelings the space to come and go, life is much more manageable, and the hard times eventually pass.

Remember, most of your suffering comes from your reaction to your feelings, not the feelings themselves.

✳

No matter how much you suffer, no matter how senseless it may seem at times, understand that life doesn't benefit from you being out of alignment. It benefits from you being *in* alignment. The world is at peace when you are at peace with yourself. All suffering is designed to strengthen your resolve to get back in sync with your inner truth. You cannot stray too far, and you cannot get lost. Suffering always reminds you to come back to being you.

BALANCE

Life is chaos unless you control it, thinks the mind. But that's only a reflection of the mind's own chaos. At some level, it knows how little it knows. And even the things it knows, it struggles to retain and organize into one cohesive truth structure. Underlying the incessant need for control is a sense of continuous overwhelm by the enormous task of making rational sense of life.

The solution is never to get better at making sense of life. Then you're just thinking harder to get through it. Rather, the solution is to come out of your tumultuous headspace altogether. You can then derive direction and purpose, not from a better understanding of life, but from experiencing yourself as a co-creator of it.

✳

To participate in life is to take part in its balance. You can see it all around you. Everything has a complementing opposite. Hot and cold. Light and dark. Happy and sad. While the exact range may vary depending on the observer, the underlying principle is clear: Whether life is expanding or contracting, the dynamic always centers around balance.

As such, everything that exists can only exist in the context of its opposite. That means nothing can be denied its purpose. Intrinsically, everything is of equal value, by virtue of its sheer existence.

Everything that exists holds space for its opposite.

Your mind, however, doesn't understand the bigger picture so readily. And even if it does, it doesn't know what to do with it. It's designed to label things in isolation, judging them as good and bad, right and wrong, fair and unfair, for the purpose of staying in control and achieving outcomes. As long as you believe your thoughts, it's no wonder you feel separate from life.

The moment you come out of your headspace, however, you realize nothing needs to be judged. Everything has a right to be. Moreover, everything is perfect the way it is. Sadness is just as valid as happiness, loss just as important as gain. Even the ability to not be you must exist, so you can choose to be you. Nothing deserves to be rejected because everything is part of the inherent balance. And by not holding on to anything, by no longer clinging and resisting, you experience this balance within you.

✳

The hardest part about your journey of self-realization is that it takes you to the darkest corners of your conditioned mind. All beliefs need to be released to free yourself and enjoy a balanced life. All of who you *think* you are must go for you to realize who you truly are.

Letting go of your mind-made truth is never easy. When parts of your truth structure dissolve, it makes you question everything. But no matter how much you feel rattled, remember that you're in the process of balancing out; that being in a dark place means learning to recognize light; that being down means you're getting ready to be on top; that feeling broken means discovering you are whole.

Feeling imbalanced fuels your expansion.

✳

To be you is to be grounded in your natural equilibrium. By respecting the balance of life, you nurture it in yourself. You realize who you are, not by becoming exceptional in some parts of you, but by becoming balanced in all of you. It's the balance of all thoughts and feelings, the full embrace of life flowing through you, that makes you complete. Be you and be all you can be.

YOUR NATURAL STATE

Whenever you experience anything in life for the first time, it's like being a child. You're fully present, full of awe, full of wonder. Your attention doesn't waver, and you're deeply immersed in the experience, not knowing what to expect next. Or rather, you're deeply immersed *because* you don't know what to expect next.

To be in awe and wonder is your natural state. You experience it whenever you encounter something new, something you have no preconception of. But you lose the wonder as soon as you start forming an opinion. Your mind takes over, and instead of responding to circumstances, you react to your existing beliefs.

Think of your home or other places you frequent. Many things have been there for so long you don't even notice them anymore. Even your favorite items, like furniture, a photograph, or art, have become virtually invisible to you.

Like a great song that grows dull after too many listens, you no longer experience things as fresh and new because your relationship is no longer with the things. It's with your mental snapshot of those things. And because all snapshots imply permanence, life grows dull, and you start taking even your most prized possessions for granted.

The same applies to the people in your life, your family, friends, partners, co-workers. You know them so well, your relationship is no longer with the person who shows up, but with who you've labeled them to be. Even when they're standing right in front of you, your beliefs override your direct experience of who they are right now.

Have you ever had someone close to you request to be called by a different name? If so, you know how weird and uncomfortable it makes you feel initially. And that's just with a name. It's exponentially more challenging to accept changes in personality. Even though everyone grows and evolves, your mind doesn't want to let go of the old images it carries.

The mind wants everything it knows to stay the same.

When you live in your head, everything gets old. Every single belief takes away a piece of the mystery of life. Without mystery, nothing remains other than what you already know. The great irony is that you try so hard to predict the future, you get so frustrated that you can't, but if everything were to go exactly according to plan, you would be bored out of your mind.

＊

Every new moment is the leading edge of life. It's where all possibilities exist and where all coming and going happens. It's the freshest, most vibrant, most powerful place you can be. It's where your life unfolds.

Life is one sparkling moment of newness after another. It's endless oohs and aahs.

Your biggest challenge in life should be keeping up with all the oohs and aahs. But when you're in your headspace, you struggle to notice even just a few. Your mind labels the current moment as *known* and immediately jumps to the next one. You never experience your natural state of awe and wonder because your mind's desire to know things gobbles up every instance of new.

Stay open to the oohs and aahs of life. Cherish each new moment, for it contains all the things that inspire. The creative genius of nature. The magnitude of life's scale. The exhilarating attention to detail. Life's endless desire to provide a thriving environment for all beings, animate and inanimate alike. Every moment contains the infinitude, the order, the beauty. Every moment contains you.

CREATIVITY

Life's creativity knows no limits. If you ever stop to watch a nature scene, you are soon mesmerized by the endless variety of shapes, colors, sounds, and smells, above the ground, below the ground, in the air, and the sea. You get the impression there's a crazy genius at play. Everything frolics about in a trance-like state. So much is going on, so much interplay between all the elements, it seems excessive, like no world needs this much abundance to sustain itself. If one thing is clear: Life *loves* to create.

You, too, are an expression of this creativity. What's more, you're free to express it in your own unique way. If there's ever a channel through which creativity loves to express itself, it's you.

Creativity is your life force.

*

But you can't be that channel when you're in your head. The rational mind is hardly creative. Its entire purpose is to eradicate the unknown. But without the unknown, the key ingredient to conceiving something genuinely original is missing. All the mind does is compare, analyze, label, define, and recombine things that already exist. Real creativity only comes from being in the flow. It can only arise from not knowing.

If you ever feel bored and uninspired, it's not because you've used up your creative juices. It's because you're in your headspace, cut off from your natural state of awe and wonder. If there's nothing left to be curious about, even your greatest passions turn into passionless routines.

But no matter how great the burnout, your creative connection is always there. You can quickly and easily turn it back on. Just a few minutes of thought awareness can remove the toughest creative block. That doesn't apply to just creative endeavors, either. Your whole life blossoms when you reconnect with the coming and going.

When you're in the flow, life is a work of art.

*

To be you is to be connected to the source of all creativity. The more connected you are, the more certain you become that no challenge exists you can't find the answer to. No downturn can stop you from getting back on your feet. No situation can overwhelm you because you're so much bigger than any one situation. Be a masterpiece. Be you.

FREEDOM

Everybody wants freedom. Freedom from the demands of everyday life, freedom to do the things you love, freedom to do nothing at all; freedom from health issues, relationship stress, financial worries; freedom from others telling you what to do.

In the quest for freedom, your first impulse is to get away from the people, places, and things you feel restricted by. You might avoid a neighbor who annoys you or work late to get out of social responsibilities. And when things get too crowded, you might look for a new job, move to a new city, or - somewhat paradoxically - get into a new relationship. And then there's the most common strategy of all, which is to work harder doing what you don't like now, to make more money, so you can be free to do the things you do like then. This approach is socially sanctioned and is better known as *retirement*.

Certainly, setting boundaries and taking clear action is necessary to create the space for you to blossom. But while creating space around you is important, you forget that the far greater restrictions are the ones you put on yourself. Your biggest limitations are your beliefs that freedom comes from achieving certain outcomes. That demanding love from others leads to loving yourself. That you can avoid discomfort by pushing away your feelings. And that the world is here to make you happy. You expect all those things to make you feel complete - when all you need to realize is that you already are.

*

You can rearrange the circumstances of your life all you want. As long as you look to your environment to save you, you keep re-creating the same limiting situations as before. You cannot become freer by changing the world around you. Your circumstances may change, but your reactions are the same.

Ultimately, circumstances don't dictate how you feel. How you respond to your circumstances dictates how you feel.

True freedom comes from no longer making the world responsible for your happiness. Only then life is free to come and go, without you judging the coming and going. And without mental judging to cloud your senses, you are free to listen to your inner voice.

*

The biggest obstacle to attaining true freedom is the fear of losing yourself when you're asked to let go of who you think you are. Of course, who you think you are is just your mind talking, but that doesn't make the fear any less real. In fact, letting go of beliefs *is* the fear. Your past, your future, your whole truth structure, have been long in the making. Your headspace has become your headquarters. So much so, that a few seconds of thought awareness cause your mind to freak out because it's no longer free to think about all those other things.

*

As you become more aware of your thoughts, your self-limiting beliefs fall away and you no longer feel like anything is missing. You feel less triggered because you respond more and react less. You don't need to prove yourself because you *are* yourself. You don't fear the unknown because you're not giving it your attention. You're no longer held back by thoughts of what *could* happen because you no longer believe your thoughts.

There comes a point when you realize you're not contracting by letting go of your beliefs, you're expanding. You're not giving up on outcomes, you're releasing limitations. You're not planning less, you're inviting more. You're not taking away from who you are, you're taking away from who you're not.

✳

Lack of freedom comes from expecting the world to make up for what you're missing within.

The fewer expectations you have, the freer you become.

If you're thinking now that all you have to do is stop expecting, and then you get what you want, you're still in your headspace. You're still steering. You're still attached to outcomes. This attachment is a container for all of your suffering, your anxiety, your disappointment in life. Until you let go of everything you believe, you cannot be truly happy, complete, and free.

There's no greater joy than doing things because you're free to do them, without the need for it to lead somewhere. That's what it means to be in the flow. That's when you're part of the coming and going. True freedom doesn't come from making life happen. It comes from letting life happen.

HEAVEN

Prayer, chanting, rituals, and meditation are just a few of the countless practices that have been an essential part of human evolution since the dawn of time.

Without a doubt, incorporating devotional elements into your life can have an immensely positive impact on your outlook and well-being. You get to nurture a side of you that is bigger than just your concept of self. You get to come out of your anxious headspace and experience a more connected state with yourself, others, and the world.

But the pull of your mind always looms large. It seeks to rationalize and intellectualize your practice, turning the aspirational and allegorical into the prescriptive and literal. It turns wisdom that is meant to unify into mental concepts that bring about separateness. Quickly, devotion becomes yet another control mechanism of the mind to reinforce getting the life you want and not the one you don't.

To step into your highest power is to become aware of your thoughts. It is to recognize that all the imperfections you see in the world stem from the imperfect image you have of yourself. To experience life's perfection, you must first honor your own. To see life's beauty, you must first see it in yourself.

When you love yourself, you love life.

✳

Life wants nothing more than for you to be you. When you get off track, it compels you to get back on. When you feel broken, it fuels your desire to be whole. When you feel lost, all it takes is a single instance of being you to feel at home again.

Everything is designed to help you realize who you are. All you're being asked to do is participate in the endless diversity and beautiful impossibility of your existence. You are meant to thrive and become invigorated by the awe and wonder of each new moment, bringing with it the essence of the infinite creativity from which you arise. You are pushed to recognize the immense love, care, and perfection that has gone into your blueprint - while continuously being reminded that you really don't know anything and that pretending you do is what's making you crazy. You get to live a life where everything you could ever imagine - and so much more that you can't - reveals itself on its own, if only you let it.

*

There is no greater feeling than being in sync with life; to feel your heart beat with the original of all intentions; to recognize the truth that is wholly your own, imparted by that which is all; to experience yourself as infinite and timeless as the ever-expanding cosmos; to feel yourself as radiant as the ever-brilliant sun; to get to love life alongside life loving you.

And for that blink-of-an-eye moment that you inhabit space and time, in the endless expanse of all that has been and continues to be created, before that which grants you life claims you back, you get to be you. What a gift. What an honor. To be you is to be in heaven.

MIRACLES

Miracles are events deemed so unusual, they defy all logic and rationale. But just because you can't make rational sense of something doesn't make it unusual. Just because you've never heard of it before doesn't mean it can't happen. Just because you label something *impossible* doesn't make it any less likely.

Everything is possible, all the time. The only limits that exist are your beliefs.

✳

The world is so much more complex than any one person can comprehend. Your life experience is but a tiny fraction of the infinite potential of the whole. You cannot begin to track what's possible for you. Yet, that's precisely what you attempt to do when you live in your head: make sense of life. More specifically, make sense of *your* life.

Your mind generates the past and the future, hopes and desires, goals and outcomes, your entire truth structure, your identity, your filtered reality - so much extra stuff that would otherwise not exist.

Life's so simple when you don't try to control it. It's so confusing and complicated when you do.

It's only in the context of your mind's obsession with control that a *miracle* is even a thing. Once you stop believing that you understand life, there are no standout events to call *miracles* because all of life is a miracle. Every moment is. Life doesn't operate in *non-miracle* mode, only to be interrupted by miracles now and then. To label one thing as miraculous is to negate the phenomenon of everything in existence. You're taking everything you don't call a miracle for granted.

✳

Nothing that exists can be discounted. Not being you is just as perfect as being you. Feeling lost is just as valuable as finding yourself. Even your entire filtered reality needs to be embraced for what it is. Ultimately, every single thought you have is a miracle - even if it's fraught with fear, even if it's just a projection, even when it interrupts the flow. Your ability to recognize the miracle around you depends on how open you are to see it within you. The more you are in awe of being you, the more you are in awe of life.

There is so much to be in awe about. One doesn't know where to begin. To live in a world that mirrors how you see yourself is beyond extraordinary. How everything stays in balance is beyond comprehension. From the stars to the planets, down to every grain of sand, and all living beings in between, the coordination between the elements *must* be spectacular for you to be able to wake up to the rising sun every morning. The totality of everything that exists, as it is contained in every new moment, is a miracle in every sense of the word. And that includes you.

Stay connected to the feeling of the miraculous you. Every single breath is a chance to feel it, sustain it, honor it. Be the miracle. Be you.

THE THREE ROADS

There are three roads on your journey of self-realization.

The first road is *The Long Road*. This is where you continue to react blindly to your environment without ever reflecting on why things manifest the way they do. You don't see the lesson contained in everything that happens. You only see things not happening the way you want them to. You stay in resistance to whatever you don't understand and whatever doesn't match your expectations. You never let go of your identity or question your beliefs, and you never come out of your headspace long enough to realize you're in it - and that you don't need to be.

The Long Road is an endless emotional roller coaster. You're consumed by clinging to the feelings you like and resisting the ones you don't. You're at odds with a world that is constantly interfering with your plans. You hardly achieve any outcomes because you're so busy reacting.

The Long Road is the hardest road because you're in
constant resistance to the flow. You never stop steering and
controlling, so you never even catch a glimpse of the
coming and going. You lack direction and purpose, you're
never satisfied with anything you achieve, and life always
feels like it hasn't yet begun. When things don't go
according to plan it hits you *hard*. Life keeps challenging
you to release stuck feelings, but you keep holding on to
them. You're unaware that the world is your mirror and
that it's you who's in the driver's seat of your evolution.

Eventually, of course, life *does* pry your fingers off the
steering wheel. It's just a very long road. That said, on the
scale of infinity, your resistance to the flow is barely a blip.
Sooner or later, you're bound to let go of your self-limiting
beliefs. You're bound to be who you're meant to be. You're
bound to experience heaven.

*

The second road is *The Middle Road*. You still react to the
world blindly, you still hang on to your feelings, and you
still make decisions based on fear and attachment to
outcome. Conditioned behaviors and ingrained beliefs
continue to rule your life, and you live for the day when the
things you want bring you the fulfillment you're missing.
But there's one big difference: When the things you want
don't deliver the fulfillment you expect, you make peace
with it. Instead of continuing to insist on your version of
life, you accept the version that presents itself.

At first, it can be a harsh awakening when the life you find yourself in doesn't match the life you've envisioned. But eventually, you let go of your expectations and settle into the reality in front of you. This results in a softening of the controlling mind and a release of stuck feelings.

Gradually, it sinks in that letting go of expectations doesn't mean living with disappointment. On the contrary, it means discovering that true fulfillment is an inner state that comes from non-resistance to life, that your happiness doesn't depend on creating ideal circumstances, and that whichever road your life may take, every one of them is as magical and rewarding as the next.

Of course, there is still much hardship on *The Middle Road* because your attachments must first become your reality for you to be able to make peace with them. But when you do, you emerge a wiser, more grounded person who is aware of the patterns of stuck feelings from which your circumstances have manifested. In other words, on *The Middle Road* you learn your lessons.

With each new lesson, your insistence on living the life you imagine diminishes. You're more likely to accept your reality as it happens because you've learned that resisting what has already happened is futile. There is a growing sense that happiness doesn't come from steering but from relinquishing control; that joy can be found in each and every situation; and that a fulfilling life is all about the art of letting it unfold.

*

The third road is *The No Road*. You're aware that the world is your mirror and that everything you experience points back to yourself. You know that clinging and resisting only keeps you trapped in your headspace, cut off from your inner voice, and lost to your inner truth.

But most importantly, your learning curve no longer consists of chasing plans, insisting on outcomes, and then having to make peace with life when it happens differently. Instead, you recognize that stuck feelings are at the root of everything you manifest and that you can come out of your suffering by learning to release them *now*, without having to go through the painful experiences they create.

This road is called *The No Road* because when you no longer blame the past or project into the future, when you no longer cling to your beliefs of who you are, something spectacular happens: Your identity collapses, time fades away, and your expectations for the next moment dissolve.

And that's when you realize - there is no road. There is nowhere you need to get to. There is no one you need to become. It's not about healing because you're already whole. It's not about becoming complete because you already are. It's not even about letting your life unfold. You realize *you are life unfolding*.

∗

Everyone's journey of self-realization is a combination of *The Three Roads*. In some areas of life, you might continue to resist, while in others, you make peace with your reality.

In other areas, still, you experience the flow of things coming and going. Where the balance of your life falls is entirely up to you.

If you keep reacting to the world from stuck feelings, you continue to experience a mix of *The Long Road* and *The Middle Road*. There's nothing wrong with that. There's nothing wrong with anything in life. All roads lead to you.

But by taking *The No Road*, you're in the fast lane of your journey of self-realization. Not that you can expect to reach the finish line sooner - there is none. There is no final destination. There is only being you now.

Being you now is your highest calling. It's the reason you exist. You take the light of your inner alignment with you wherever you go. It extends to everyone around you, all who have gone before, and all who are yet to come. Your light has no limits, knows no time. It can only grow bigger and brighter.

Keep doing, learning, growing. There are no conditions or situations that can prevent you from realizing yourself more. In fact, it's the conditions and situations that take you there.

Your inner voice is here to guide you, patiently and steadfastly. Life itself is a great big mirror that does everything to reveal your path. You cannot get lost, for the love of creation wants you to be you. It wants you to know you're already as perfect as can be. And to recognize it, all you're being asked to do is fall in love with yourself. What a beautiful design.

IDENTITY

You've come so far and learned so much. You understand the difference between judgment and non-judgment, resistance and non-resistance, filtered and unfiltered reality. You understand the true meaning of suffering, forgiveness, and self-love, and that most of your confusion comes from using your mind for something it's not designed to do. You're aware of your inner voice and how being in your headspace cuts you off from it. You recognize the purpose of triggers, the benefits of releasing stuck feelings, and the importance of taking clear action. You're more aware than ever of your fully realized self.

But how are you able to discern all of these states? If you can feel the difference between being in your head versus being in your body, then you must be independent of both. If you can tell when you're being you, and when not, then you must be neither. If all thoughts and feelings come and go, then you are not your thoughts and feelings. You are not your doubts and fears, or even your joy and happiness. You are not who you think you are, who you hope to be, or who you remember yourself as. You are not any of the labels and concepts you attach your sense of self to. So then, *who are you?*

✳

As stuck feelings leave you, the limited view they impose on your sense of self does, too. It becomes clear that your entire identity is an elaborate mosaic of opinions about yourself. To say *this is who I am*, and *this is who I'm not*, is to reduce yourself to a handful of limiting beliefs that make up the core of your truth structure. This core identity is a tiny spec of all that is possible. No wonder your mind makes you feel small and helpless when you're confronted by life. You're working with the most limited toolbox, unaware that your true self is so much bigger than your circumstances; bigger than your triggers; bigger than your judgments; bigger than your suffering.

You're so much bigger than you think you are.

✳

The more you let go of your beliefs, the freer you become. You no longer make the world responsible for how you feel. You no longer chase your future happiness because you're connected to the miracle of every moment that's already here. By letting all feelings come and go, you invite more abundance than ever to enter your field of experiences. With each passing feeling, you're reminded of the infinite creativity you're a part of, and that the rational mind can never begin to comprehend how limitless you really are.

Your journey of self-realization is a march towards your limitlessness. No matter how bumpy the road may be at times, you can only move forward, never back. As your self-limiting beliefs fall away, so does your self-image of *me*. You find yourself no longer able to fit into the mold others have set for you. The world's demands to define who you are, what you believe in, what you want, leave you staring with a blank face. A dim memory of your old life of opinions and conditioned beliefs may still exist - but you know you can never go back.

You've reached a tipping point where *not* knowing who you are *is* your new identity. Certain personal traits - such as your name, job title, where you live - remain as part of staying functional in a head-centric world. But beyond the organizational, you have become too fluid for any thoughts and feelings to remain static. You're expanding faster than any beliefs about *me* can take hold. Or rather, you're expanding *because* any beliefs about *me* are not getting stuck.

It's scary at first when you realize your new identity is not having one. But don't worry, you get used to it.

Continuous expansion is your natural state.

*

Continuous expansion is what it means to be in the flow. When you don't hold on to anything, there is nothing left for you to form a rigid identity from. Not that you even try. You're no longer the *me* that attempts to bend the world to its will. You're no longer a small and lonely creature trying to make sense of a big scary world. You're no longer the sum of your attachments to all the things you want so dearly to give you meaning, to make you happy, in hopes they reflect a hint of the infinite love you carry within.

The moment you truly let go everything falls into place. Resistance gives way to flow. Separateness gives way to unity. The unknown becomes the known. The scary becomes the trustworthy. And the impermanence of life reveals your permanent, fully realized self.

All this time, you've been using your mind to create something you can believe in. And now you know: By believing nothing, you become everything. You become you.

LOVE

Experiencing the physical world is beyond mesmerizing. The process of being born is so explosive, so spectacular, so improbable. One moment you're formless, and the next, you're a conscious being in a body in the middle of an infinitely vibrant ecosystem. It's impossible to comprehend all the forces that have gone into manifesting this process. It's hard to imagine anything involving more contrast, than going from your non-physical state to the physical one.

No wonder your natural state is to be in awe. The world has so much to offer. Why wouldn't you be totally smitten by it? Why wouldn't you seek your happiness in it? You've discovered the ultimate playground. An unlimited number of experiences - of people, places, and things - is within reach. What could be more deserving of your fullest attention than the incredible world around you?

But no matter how much excitement you experience, no matter how lofty the goals you achieve, you're always left wanting more. Deep down, far beyond the reaches of the rational mind, there is a feeling that something is missing. It re-surfaces every time the fleeting satisfaction of the physical world subsides. This feeling is the longing to be loved unconditionally and accepted for who you are.

As long as you're in your headspace, all you know is to keep making plans and keep creating conditions, expecting the world to bring you the perfect love you're missing. Surely, amidst all the infinite beauty and abundance, it *must* exist somewhere?

As it turns out, it does. But not without a twist. The perfect love you long for cannot be found *in* the world around you - it is found *through* it. In fact, that's how life is designed to work. You're supposed to be hypnotized by the endless variety around you. You're supposed to pursue all the things your heart desires. You're supposed to get attached to the people, places, and things you love. It's only from a place of deep infatuation that you can learn to let go of the things and recognize the love that has gone into creating them.

There is no better way to connect to the love of creation than to connect to all that it creates.

Everything manifests from this love of creation. It's a love that knows no right or wrong. It knows no true or false. It knows everything is perfect as it exists *because* it exists. Everything that exists is full of love.

That includes you. This perfect love lives within you, too. Somewhere deep inside, at the root level, you carry an ancient imprint of the passion for creation you're made of. It's the place where your deepest longing emanates from. It's where you know you're not alone. It's where you come out of separateness, no longer a stranger to the flow.

＊

Your journey is to connect to the love of continuous creation, of life coming and going. It's a love that knows no boundaries and has no limits. It's the love you emerge from and the love you return home to.

The great adventure of life lies before you. It has your full self-realization at heart. You always manifest the next set of circumstances that help you realize yourself more. There are no uncertainties. There is no delay. Life rewards you instantly for being you.

Realizing who you are is your journey, much more than a final destination. If there is an end to your existence, it's on the scale of suns and galaxies. In the meantime, every breath you take is an opportunity to be more of you.

Life has your back. Your inner voice leads the way. You are meant to be happy, free, and limitless. You already are. You just have to realize it.

Be happy. Be free. Be you.

The Practice
of Being You

4 STEPS TO BE YOU

1
Practice Thought Awareness
...to come out of your headspace

2
Observe and Release Stuck Feelings
...to come out of blind reactivity

3
Listen to Your Inner Voice
...to align with the flow of life

4
Take Clear Action
...to realize yourself more

4 STEPS TO BE YOU

1
Practice Thought Awareness
...to come out of your headspace

2
Observe and Release Stuck Feelings
...to come out of blind reactivity

3
Listen to Your Inner Voice
...to align with the flow of life

4
Take Clear Action
...to realize yourself more

4 STEPS
TO BE YOU

1
Practice Thought Awareness
...to come out of your headspace

2
Observe and Release Stuck Feelings
...to come out of blind reactivity

3
Listen to Your Inner Voice
...to align with the flow of life

4
Take Clear Action
...to realize yourself more

Made in the USA
Las Vegas, NV
25 February 2023

68154784R00156